ANATOMY OF ANTI-COMMUNISM

ANATOMY OF ANTI-COMMUNISM

ANATOMY OF
ANTI-COMMUNISM

*A Report Prepared for the
Peace Education Division of the
American Friends Service Committee*

HILL AND WANG • NEW YORK

First Edition January 1969

Manufactured in the United States of America by
The Colonial Press Inc., Clinton, Massachusetts
2   3   4   5   6   7   8   9   10

PROLOGUE: The Realistic—and the Right

THERE IS A FAITH that a man, any man, has infinite worth. Social organization is a means to an end. The end is the welfare not of abstract Man but of every man anywhere and therefore of all men everywhere; for all men are created equal and endowed by their Creator with certain inalienable rights. This is a faith; it is not demonstrable.

This faith—humanistically or theistically expressed—animates the American Friends Service Committee and informs its work and days. The Committee asked the authors of this study to prepare an analysis of anti-Communism. The authors have labored under the burden of the Committee's faith. That faith underlies the arguments advanced here; without it, the arguments are irrelevant to the human situation.

The arguments we make are essentially strategic. As we see it, a blind, fanatical anti-Communism is and has been disadvantageous to our country and its people. It has not "stopped Communism"; it has not advanced human liberty abroad or at home.

We believe that other men's motives are no worse than our own. We assume that all men everywhere would like to be just and deal justly—and that they are deflected from this high impulse by the consideration that it would be unprofitable for them to do so.

The United States is fortunate, then, when the *right* course can be seen as the *strategic* or advantageous one.

That occasion seems to be upon us, for the first time in history. Something has "got into" the people who for some aeons have lived at or below a human subsistence level, both economically and politically. The world's advantaged minority is incapable any longer of ruling, much less exploiting, the disadvantaged majority. An equitable distribution of economic and political opportunity has always been right; the pressures toward such a distribution are now increasing rapidly.

Our country and its people have been fortunate. We have not had to have a colonial empire, and we have been spared the moral disaster of having one. We ourselves are the beneficiaries of our own "war of national liberation." We have helped millions of the world's wretched to their feet by opening our doors to them. Of all people, we should be most able to understand why those whom modernization has left behind have suddenly resolved to protest against their own suffering.

But the Communist has a case against the Western world as the Western world has a case against him. We point to his imposition —or perpetuation—of political servitude. He points to parliamentary capitalism's perpetuation of economic misery. Those in misery cry "Bread," and as long as they do not have bread they do not, and will not, respond to our slogan of "Liberty."

Our faith requires Christians to understand the Communist. *Strategy* requires us, if not to love Communists, at least to treat them as if we loved them. The strategic statement of the case has been made in cryptic fashion: The alternatives are co-existence or no existence. So too, in the "long, hot summers" of the 1960's, many white Americans began to realize that the right thing to do about the Negro ghettos was also the thing that had to be done lest our country be ruined by civil war.

But the authors of this study would not here urge our countrymen to do what they believe is right because it is advantageous. We would urge instead a venture of faith, and a dedication of energy, of knowledge, and of riches to the relief of human want, not because it stops Communism, but because it stops starvation and despair— because it is right.

The consideration of the practical tends always to overwhelm the consideration of the moral in all of us. There is no point in bemoaning the limitations of our human nature; that is the way men are, and that is the way that we are. When we have recognized that the moral and the strategic are identical—and that we are relieved of truly painful moral choice—we have put ourselves into the treacherous hands of the strategic. When, then, the two divide, or appear to, we are tempted to abandon the former for the latter. The single abiding necessity then is to do the right thing, regardless of the consequences to us or our country.

The need now is not to "stop Communism"—or to go on trying in vain to do so by military means—but to see the good in it as well as the bad and to see the failures of capitalism, even of enlightened capitalism, as we now see the good. To change our own course in the direction of all-out social justice is the right thing to do. And it must be done. Anti-Communism, in one form or another, has been tried, and tried, and tried—and has failed. The ultimate penalty of doctrinaire anti-Communism is our own destruction—along with that of the Communists.

Members of the Working Party:

JAMES E. BRISTOL
HOLLAND HUNTER
JAMES H. LAIRD
SIDNEY LENS
MILTON MAYER
ROBERT E. REUMAN
ATHAN THEOHARIS
BRYANT WEDGE

Postscript

The disturbing invasion in August 1968 of Czechoslovakia by Warsaw Pact troops occurred after the text of this book had been prepared and sent to press. While it is still too early for adequate analysis of this continuing event, the following provisional observations seem to be warranted.

1. Whatever insecurities and provocations the Soviet leadership may have felt, its response to Czechoslovakian developments was unilateral, repressive of a peoples' emerging hopes, and deserving of condemnation.

2. The U.S.S.R., and probably the East German Democratic Republic, revealed by this response both internal tensions and insecurity with respect to Western, especially West German, nonmilitary penetration into Eastern Europe.

3. The decreasing unanimity of Eastern European countries has been underscored by the Czechoslovakian invasion, the processes of fragmentation and even polarization within that alliance greatly accelerated.

4. The invasion itself was unique in its softness, and the hesitancy of its inception, just as the resistance of the Czechs was unique in terms of its relatively nonviolent, persistent, and unified character.

5. While the Czechoslovakian invasion represents a new stage in East-West relations, it does *not* undercut the fundamental analyses and recommendations that are presented here. Rather it empha-

sizes the changing nature of Communism and East-West relations, while underscoring the importance of continuous rational assessment, mutual understanding of problems, and flexible responses.

Vietnam - p. 15
Military spending - p 50

CONTENTS

"Vietnam is the arena where Communist expansionism is most aggressively at work in the world today."

President Lyndon B. Johnson to National Legislative Conference in San Antonio, Texas, September 29, 1967

"I am compelled to the conclusion that to a large extent the move to increase trade with the Soviet Union and Eastern European countries is a matter of grave concern. . . . This is . . . only a part of the broad, continuing campaign to advance the cause of Communism throughout the world by whatever means possible. . . ."

Representative Glenard P. Lipscomb, Congressman from California, in an address before the American Management Association, March 8, 1967

"I find no significant body of American opinion which would have us withdraw from Vietnam and abandon Southeast Asia to the fate which Asian Communism has planned for it."

Dean Rusk, at a press conference, November 12, 1967

"Communism has to be stopped somewhere."

PFC Steve Stone, a GI in Vietnam, November 1967

"I'm for the war, of course, because I am against Communism."

Woman shopper in Newman, Georgia, November 22, 1967

"J. Edgar Hoover said today American Communists were finding the black power movement tailor-made to their efforts to stir up racial unrest. . . . He said Communist Party leaders were 'pleased with the disturbances on campuses and the disruption of city life by war protestors and riots in the ghettos.' "

The New York Times, January 6, 1968. From J. Edgar Hoover's Annual Report to the Attorney General, Washington, January 5, 1968

INTRODUCTION

A FEW YEARS AGO a distinguished French journalist, returning home after a lecture tour in the United States, was asked what most profoundly impressed him there. He replied: "The fact that in America a man can get away with saying absolutely anything, no matter how trivial, preposterous, obscene, or even treasonable, providing he begins and ends by saying 'I hate Communism.'"

Anti-Communism has become The American Way, the admission ticket to respectability. Whatever else a man may or may not be, he has the possibility of a popular following if, like the late Senator Joseph R. McCarthy, he is a sleepless anti-Communist. A common criminal once defended himself by invoking this single credential. Even liberal statesmen have often relied on it to make themselves acceptable to their constituencies. In the summer of 1954, Senator Hubert Humphrey, a candidate for re-election, proposed an amendment to a bill that provided criminal penalties for membership in the Communist Party. When his amendment was deleted as too sweeping, Senator Humphrey told the Senate: "These rats are not going to get out of this trap. We have slammed the door on them, and if this law is not strong enough to do the whole job, I will come back next year to help make it stronger, if I am re-elected." [1]

The strident character of anti-Communist pronouncements has been replaced in recent years by a more enlightened stance. Except for a relatively small minority on the extreme right the McCarthyist technique is now passé. Anti-Communism became institutionalized through the enactment of various local, state, and national laws intended to restrict both the political and subversive activities of Communists, but the courts have modified the hysteria hardened into law by outlawing some sections of the Internal Security Act of 1950 and by upholding the right to dissent. Since Tito's defection and the subsequent polycentric developments in the Communist world, the common American attitude to individual Communist nations has been somewhat modified. We refer to the U.S.S.R in tones that differ from those we use for Communist

[1] *The New York Times,* August 20, 1954.

China, and we distinguish Communist Poland from Communist Albania.

If an American President, at the height of the McCarthy era, had declared it our national policy to "build bridges" between ourselves and the Soviets, he would have been driven from office. But now the United States builds bridges with guarded enthusiasm, originally to the Communist dissenters in Yugoslavia, now to the whole European Communist world. Americans can do business with them, the government says; but the Chinese are something else again. In addition to being Communists, they are Orientals, not Caucasians. In our attitude toward Communist China, racism may be a factor. Overt or covert, it may influence our "quarantine" of a fourth of the world's population and our implacable struggle to keep them out of the United Nations.

So the policy of building bridges proceeds hand in glove with the contrary policy of stopping Communism wherever we can or however we can, and even of fighting the Russians under the table. They supply aid to our enemies, and we to theirs; and we continue to build bridges. At the same time, our government's only answer to the question, "Why Vietnam?" is, "We have to stop Communism." The substance of a reflex anti-Communism persists.

Anti-Communism colors every facet of American policy. It has become an almost unconscious habit of mind; it is assumed almost without debate. Our national likes and dislikes are colored by it. We have evolved a double set of standards, which says that when *they* do something, it is evil; but when *we* do the same thing, it is necessary for self-defense or for national security. This double standard is no more clear than in our attitudes toward the Soviet invasion of Czechoslovakia in August 1968. This was roundly condemned almost unanimously by Americans, most of whom would not weigh the United States war in Vietnam on the same scale, although both the United States and the U.S.S.R. were motivated by the desire to maintain in power a government which was acceptable.

The forms have changed, but the character has set. Anti-Communism in our country is an endemic state of panic. Henry Steele Commager, the dean of contemporary American historians, says that "there has come up in recent years, particularly since the coming of the Cold War, something that might be called a conspiracy psychology—a feeling that great events cannot be explained by ordinary processes. I think we've been persuaded very largely to be more receptive to conspiracy theories. I don't think we've become paranoid, but we are on the road to a paranoid explanation of things."

So, too, Eric Sevareid, the Columbia Broadcasting System commentator, says that "the devil theory is prevalent in American politics. Roosevelt must have sold out at Yalta. Obscure Reds in the State Department must have delivered vast China into Communist hands. Roosevelt must have conspired with the Japanese to bring about the attack on Pearl Harbor. . . ."

How did this devil theory of anti-Communism come about? What is it? What is its purpose?

The first fact that is obvious to objective scrutiny is that anti-Communism operates at two levels—within the public at large and within the government. At the public level it is primarily an unthinking response of fear; at the government level it is more a genuine anxiety that is willing to exploit the public fear and use it to win support for military and economic policies not necessarily related to the question of Communism.

The fear of the American people was intensified following World War II, partially through disclosures about forced-labor camps in Siberia. After the Soviet Union became part of the western alliance, Poles captured in 1939, when the Soviet armies occupied Eastern Poland, were released from Siberia under pressure from the Polish government-in-exile and Great Britain. Some of these prisoners, such as Elinor Lipper in her *Eleven Years in Soviet Prison Camps* and Dr. Jerzy Glicksman in his *Tell the West,* described experiences that horrified the American public.

It soon became apparent that millions of Russians and other East European people had been held in forced-labor camps by Stalin. Citizens of the United States were justifiably outraged. They recalled Stalin's famous purge trials of the 1930's, which liquidated thousands of those who were active in the 1917 revolution, virtually the whole leadership apart from Stalin. That men like Bukharin, Zinoviev, Kamenev, and the exiled Trotsky could now be called traitors undermined previous visions of justice and concern for individuals in the Soviet Union, and showed only frame-ups of political opponents. The role of the secret police, the incredible adulation of Stalin by the Soviet press, the total control of the unions by the State—all these confirmed a popular hostility to Communism in the United States. This hostility had existed in the 1920's and 1930's, but it was not then as intense as it was to become after World War II.

The American Communist Party, too, was seen in an ominous light, simply as an agent of a foreign power, an agent that shifted position on a number of occasions in tune with the needs of Soviet policy. It had opposed World War II as an "imperialist war" when Stalin entered into his pact with Hitler in September 1939, but it called the war a "people's war" when Hitler turned on his ally and invaded Soviet territory in June 1941. Its zig-zags indicated that the Communist Party in America was less interested in progressive principles to improve the plight of the downtrodden in the United States than in machinations that meshed its program with the political policies of another state.

To the American public, Communism was harsh, brutal, deceptive, and manipulatory. It was not difficult then for those in power to cater to that hostility, inflame it, and use it. Even when more moderate Communists took the helm in the Soviet Union—Khrushchev, Brezhnev—and reversed or jettisoned many of Stalin's policies, the original image of a monolithic and terroristic regime was sustained. This position became frozen in the American mind and for the most part resistant to reasonable analysis or change.

But if popular hostility to Communism has roots in actual conditions that prevailed in the Soviet orbit during the Stalin era, the American government's position has been based on considerations of national power. It has never been credible that the United States was opposing Communism merely because it was "totalitarian." Many of Washington's allies who comprise the so-called Free World have unfortunately been thoroughly totalitarian: Chiang Kai-shek in China, Syngman Rhee in Korea, Salazar in Portugal, the Shah of Iran, the leaders of Thailand, and half or more of the governments of Latin America, to name some. The government's anti-Communism has reflected other interests and purposes, principally a desire to prevent international changes that would unsettle the established order, cut off vast areas from the investment of United States capital, and create a global economic environment not dependent upon Western trade. The people resisted Communism for emotional reasons, the government for power reasons. But the two became blurred as McCarthyism and other forms of anti-Communist agitation transformed sound objections into a phobia. Postwar administrations were, therefore, able to pursue an antirevolutionary policy abroad without serious domestic challenge.

Not that the men who make state policy are malevolent or evil-intentioned. But they are the custodians of institutions that through the decades have been fashioned to defend those interests which are subsumed under the heading "establishment." That defense has become automatic or virtually so, and it has suggested to these officials the necessity of an anti-Communist policy in the present period. Only enlightened leadership could have overcome this handicap, but that enlightened leadership has not been forthcoming.

The consequences of this unhappy convergence have been, on the one hand, the evolution and perpetuation of many myths about the Communist and neutralist world and, on the other hand, the strengthening of those forces within the United States and abroad that stand most firmly against social change. These two aspects of anti-Communism have reinforced each other.

It is not that Communism is good; for history, in fact, shows that it has veered away in practice from its humanitarian ideals. The authors of this study criticize Communism; and, likewise, we challenge the system under which we live when it does not live up to its own ideals; but we do not consider anti-Communism to be the *opposite* of Communism. As it has developed, anti-Communism has become a political strategy that fights not only Communism, but neutralism and democratic revolution as well. It is based on antipathy to social change and a defense of the status quo—or at least as much of the status quo as can be salvaged. It utilizes fear of Communism, as a camouflage for conservative and, on occasion, reactionary policy.

We propose here to analyze this phenomenon of anti-Communism: its sources, its content, its historical origins, its role in American life. First, the origins of the anti-Communist outlook are described; second, its leading themes; next, its consequences in American domestic affairs and foreign policy. Then an effort is made to separate the Communist reality from the myth. Finally, preferable attitudes and alternatives are suggested.

ANATOMY OF ANTI-COMMUNISM

ANATOMY OF ANTI-COMMUNISM

1. HOW WE GOT THAT WAY: History of Anti-Communism[1]

THE COMMONLY ACCEPTED American explanation of the Cold War has been that this conflict was forced upon a reluctant United States. For the sake of humanity, the United States interposed its strength between an expansionist U.S.S.R. and those areas of the "free" world that the Soviet Union desired to place under its control. Only the Christian West's championship of freedom has saved humanity from global slavery. This oversimplified and fallacious reading of history has provided fuel for the anti-Communist's fiery hatred.

Attractive as the view may be to an America convinced of its own righteousness, it simply cannot be supported by historical evidence. Russian truculence is part of the picture to be sure, but only part. The facts of history indicate that blame for the Cold War is a shared guilt, and this disclosure pulls the fangs from venomous anti-Communism.

Some contemporary historians have rendered no longer tenable the uncritical acceptance of the classic view of the Cold War as a conflict in which a guiltless West is pitted against a vicious Communist foe. These historians contend, in the words of Gar Alperovitz, that "the Cold War cannot be understood simply as an American response to a Soviet challenge, but rather as the insidious interaction of mutual suspicions, blame for which should be shared by all." [2]

The following is a corrective attempt to set the record straight, to remind us of something we have forgotten if we ever knew. Examples of Russian intransigence are not dwelt on, for they are part of anti-Communist America's folklore, whereas the crimes of the West are less well known—in the West.

[1] Some material in this chapter is drawn from Sidney Lens, *The Futile Crusade: Anti-Communism as American Credo,* Chicago, Quadrangle Books, 1964.
[2] See Christopher Lasch, "The Cold War Revisited and Re-Visioned," *The New York Times Magazine,* January 14, 1968.

1

I

"The era of war and revolution." That phrase aptly describes the twentieth century. Two major wars and many minor ones have occurred among the great powers; innumerable revolutions have occurred *against* the great powers by former colonies seeking to achieve national liberation. Wars, by weakening the major states, have encouraged these revolutions; revolutions, by upsetting the international balance of power, have sometimes led to war.

The present Cold War, fought on the American side around the doctrine of anti-Communism, is integrally related to the war/revolution syndrome. A product of two wars and numerous revolutions, anti-Communism has failed to adjust to the power, political, or revolutionary ramifications confronting the twentieth century world. On one level, anti-Communism has imposed a uniformity on the Communist world and thus reduced options for maneuver. On the other hand, anti-Communism has failed to adjust to the revolution of rising expectations. And anti-Communism has not learned the folly of trying to suppress this revolution, so its international strategy is essentially a strategy of military containment and roll-back.

In the nineteenth century the advanced nations occupied most of the underdeveloped countries not already colonized and reduced them to colonial status. The result was a commitment to the retention of these territories and the exploitation of their resources. This policy required the abortion of nationalist revolutions. The British had encouraged India, for instance, to rebel against the Moguls, the Chinese to rebel against the Manchu dynasty, the Egyptians to rebel against the Ottomans, and the Latin Americans to rebel against Spain, but then the British subverted the ensuing revolutions and re-established feudal and semifeudal relationships under a veneer of capitalism. The divisions within these societies and their weakness made this policy of suppression relatively simple in the nineteenth century. It took only two thousand troops for France to bring large parts of Indochina to its knees, only fifty thousand for England to quell the aspirations of India. Anti-nationalist policy seemed secure as the twentieth century opened.

The century began with the Boxer Rebellion of 1900, following in the wake of Japan's lightning victory over China in 1894–95. Not simply a peasant revolt seeking to alleviate the lot of the village poor, the rebellion aimed at ousting British, French, German, Russian, Japanese, and American foreigners. The great powers succeeded in crushing the rebellion and imposed a $325 million indemnity on the frustrated Chinese nation.[3]

The important Mexican Revolution of 1910 and Dr. Sun Yat-sen's revolution in China the following year caused only a ripple of excitement in the corridors of Western power, since neither of these upheavals was able to consolidate itself quickly. Mexico went through a period of harrowing struggle from 1910 to 1917 followed by tumultuous indecisiveness until 1934. American reaction was confined to a few military missions, such as the seizure of Vera Cruz, and a more consistent policy of diplomatic and behind-the-scenes pressure. The Sun Yat-sen revolt seemed to be contained within South China, the war lords allied with the West, and Japan remained paramount in the North. The advanced powers were not able to interest themselves in social change—the Peace Treaty Conference of 1919 only confirmed Japan's depredations—and these powers felt no necessity for strong measures against the weak Kuomintang. Following the death of Dr. Sun, the great nations again breathed easily; for after 1927 Sun's successor, Chiang Kai-shek, adopted an anti-Communist policy. The great powers, content with the status quo, were insensitive to the fires raging beneath the surface.

The traumatic shock for the old order and a new dimension for great power politics came with the Russian Revolution of 1917; it was a shock from which the United States has never recovered. The revolution occurred in two stages; the first one, in February, was welcomed by the West as a step toward competent government capable of effectively waging the war; the second one—unanticipated in London, Paris, or Washington—was feared, shunned, and fought.

It is important to note, in digesting the lesson for the future, that Russia in 1917 was a military cipher and an economic shambles. Of the twelve million Russian troops in World War I, 76 per cent were dead, wounded, prisoners, or deserters. The Russian army had virtually disintegrated; Russia's industry and railroads were immobilized or destroyed. Hunger was rampant. It was inconceivable that Russia could be a military force of serious consequence, yet she was able to overcome military encirclement and attack by no less than fourteen foreign armies including five

[3] The U.S. indemnity was nearly $25 million, about $18 million of which was remitted to and used by China for scholarships to Chinese students for study in America. The good will generated by this act was later dissipated.

4 ANATOMY OF ANTI-COMMUNISM

hundred Americans sent to Archangel, Russia's Valley Forge. She prevailed over these armies as well as over a sizable counter-revolutionary force inside the country, astutely using social power against military power.

The Bolsheviks, let it be noted, did not initiate or lead the original revolution; in February they were merely secondary actors. The two new levers of power, the Provisional Government and the Soviets (workers' and soldiers' councils) were both for some months in the hands of others. The allied nations, however, insisted that a war-weary Russia honor its Czar's pledge to fight to the end, and when the Provisional Government abjectly concurred, it wrote its epitaph. It was Lenin's promise of "peace, bread, land," not his Communism or Marxist doctrine, that spoke to the deepest needs of a tired people willing to break with the past.

At this critical juncture, there were voices of moderation— William C. Bullitt, Lincoln Steffens, Colonel Raymond Robins in the United States; Bruce Lockhart, George Buchanan, Lord Lansdowne in England—urging a modus vivendi with Lenin and Trotsky. The belligerent faction, typified by Winston Churchill and Georges Clemenceau, was convinced that military force was necessary if the world was not to be plunged into anarchy and the British and French empires toppled. Thus originated both anti-Communism and the now famous "domino theory," neither of which proved an adequate diagnosis of the situation.

"We may well be," Churchill wrote to Lloyd George, "within measurable distance of universal collapse and anarchy throughout Europe and Asia." "No real harmony is possible between Bolshevism and present civilization"; on the contrary, "the baby," he said, "must be strangled in its crib." [4] For Churchill, the defense of the colonial empire in 1918–20 required the destruction of the Bolshevik revolution. His anti-Communism stemmed from his attachment to the imperial status quo. His strategic concepts were no wider than those of the British government that had throttled the Boxer Rebellion—military force, more military force, and still more military force.

Neither Churchill nor any of the other anti-Communist theorists seemed to understand the inner vitality of a revolution; yet it convincingly proved itself. Trotsky, by appealing to the patriotism of former Czarist officers, was able to enlist thirty thousand to forge a moderately effective Red Army. By distributing land to the peasants, Lenin was able to win them for his guerrilla forces.

[4] Lewis Broad, *Winston Churchill: A Biography*, p. 186.

Wherever the Red Army went, it took land from the landlords and gave it to the tillers of the soil; wherever the White Army went, it reversed the process, retrieving the land for its former rich owners. It should be noted that distribution of individual holdings was not a Bolshevik program: The Marxists believed in co-operatives and state farms. But they adopted a formula proclaimed by more moderate parties in order to achieve popular support. By doing so they eroded their adversaries' power and emerged victorious. By 1920 the Bolsheviks had won the Civil War and forced the allied nations, except for Japan, to withdraw. Anti-Communism's first venture had ended in fiasco.

Parenthetically, it is worth recording that anti-Communism in foreign relations at this time was accompanied in the United States by what was later to become known as McCarthyism. Those who counseled moderation in dealing with the Soviet Union were castigated as "Reds," a process as stultifying of rational debate and analysis then as it has been recently. Senator Robert M. LaFollette of Wisconsin was called a "Bolshevik spokesman in America" when he proposed withdrawal of American troops from Archangel. Colonel Raymond Robins was labeled a "Red" when he denied that Lenin and Trotsky, as rumor had it, were "German agents." Even organizations such as the Federal Council of Churches and the Foreign Policy Association were denounced, together with humanitarians such as Jane Addams and conservatives such as Charles Evans Hughes.

On the second anniversary of the Revolution, November 7, 1919, the Department of Justice carried out a series of raids, from one end of the country to the other, against radicals of various hues. Five hundred were arrested in Boston, thousands more in New York, Philadelphia, Chicago, Detroit, St. Louis. Hundreds of foreign-born were deported as dangerous leftists. On January 7, 1920, five socialists elected to the New York legislature were expelled on the grounds that their position was "inimical to the best interests of the state." A right-wing socialist elected to the Congress was denied his seat.

Nor did the failure of the initial policy of intervening in Russian affairs drastically alter policy assumptions. Intervention was replaced with quarantine and isolation by the West. It would be a mistake to recognize the Soviet Union, said Secretary of State Bainbridge Colby in August 1920, because it "is determined and bound to conspire against our institutions." (The Russian Czars, interestingly enough, had given the very same reasons for refusing to recognize the United States for thirty-three years after the American Revolution.) Overtures for friendly relations were unceremoniously rejected on the grounds, according to Colby, that Russian Communism "depends, and must continue to depend upon the occurrence of revolutions in all other great civilized nations, including the U.S., which will overthrow and destroy their governments and set up Bolshevist rule in their stead." [5] This was the 1920 version of the domino theory.

In due course the revolutionary wave receded. Soviets established in Germany, Hungary, and Finland failed to survive. The revolution in Turkey did not introduce basic social change. The West, and the United States in particular, relaxed; but the folly of anti-Communism was never properly evaluated.

During the 1930's, under the leadership of President Franklin Roosevelt, a shift occurred in United States policy when it recognized the Soviet Union, although Red-baiting was not uncommon in that period. During World War II, Roosevelt sought a modus vivendi with Soviet leaders and proclaimed a policy of co-existence with the U.S.S.R. The American President, together with most liberals of the period, hoped that the same kind of tolerance toward Communists within the country could be extended on an international plane. The policy was not based on any softness toward Communism but on the hard recognition that, after the war, nationalist revolution was inevitable and that a stable peace depended upon co-operation among the great powers and on renunciation of balance-of-power politics. To guide that revolution into safe and peaceful channels would be impossible without Soviet collaboration, and, to avert another arms race or confrontation, diplomacy required an understanding of mutual interests and objectives. Indeed leading members of the Roosevelt entourage stated that without this co-existence World War III was a certainty.

II

The world that emerged from the ashes of war was about to be swept by a revolutionary tornado. President Roosevelt perhaps had this in mind when in August 1941, four months before Pearl Harbor, he induced Winston Churchill, "somewhere in the Atlantic," to sign a charter proclaiming the Allied war aims. Section 3 of that charter promised "sovereign rights of self-government . . . to those who have been forcibly deprived of them." The people of the

[5] Quoted in George F. Kennan, *Russia and the West,* p. 206.

colonies, long deprived of national independence, now had their pledge in writing from the leaders of the alliance, and Roosevelt reinforced it in private conversations with the Sultan of Morocco and others. Throughout Asia and Africa young men joined the war with the Allies convinced that once victory over Hitler had been achieved, independence would be theirs. Gandhi in India, mindful that the British had reneged on promises of self-determination following World War I, insisted on immediate fulfillment of this obligation, but elsewhere the nationalist revolutionaries, by and large, were willing to wait.

A deep strain of nationalism showed itself in World War II. In advanced countries, it was an old fashioned nationalism, against military occupation forces; in colonial lands, it was a *revolutionary nationalism* willing to fight the Axis powers, Germany, Italy, Japan, on the side of the Allies, in order to gain national freedom in the aftermath. Almost everywhere the Communists became important factors in nationalist fronts, both in the developed and underdeveloped countries. Of the five members of the Bureau of the National Council of Resistance in France, three were Communists, and of the three members of the Council's Committee of Military Action (COMAC), two were Communists. In Italy, Communists formed a partisan movement called the Garibaldini, and in March 1944 organized a general strike in Northern Italy, which Hugh Seton-Watson describes as "the most impressive action of its kind that took place at any time in Europe under Hitler's rule." Of the two resistance movements in Yugoslavia, the most dynamic was that led by the Communist, Tito, who succeeded in tying down many German divisions. The EAM (National Liberation Front) in Greece, opposing Italian and German forces, was a broad alliance of many groups in which the Communists held leadership positions. The West, including the United States, hailed these movements and gave them moral and material aid in their struggle. Communist participation was not regarded as a handicap.

Similar developments were taking place in Asia. In Burma, an Anti-Fascist People's Freedom League under the leadership of a non-Communist was made up of Socialists, Communists, and Buddhists, resisting Japan. In Indochina, guerrilla warfare against the Japanese was waged by two groups, the most significant one being an alliance of a dozen forces headed by a native Communist, Ho Chi Minh, who had led an abortive revolt against France in 1930. In Indonesia the movement of Sukarno and Hatta included both official Communists and dissident Communists such as the late Tan

Malaka, who severed relations with Moscow before Tito did. (The present foreign minister of Indonesia, Adam Malik, was one of Tan Malaka's followers.) Virtually all such groups—certainly Ho Chi Minh's—received support and supplies from the United States. They were never criticized for being "Communist infiltrated." Indeed, President Roosevelt had sought during the war to prevent United States military effort or aid from being used to re-establish colonial rule even to the point of refusing aid to the French in Indochina in their fight against the Japanese. This policy resulted in difficult relations with our coalition Allies, the English, French, and the Dutch. After the war the United States did not put the same pressure on the French as it did on the Dutch in Indonesia to make peace with the local nationalists. Even in China, where Mao Tsetung and Chiang Kai-shek had agreed jointly to fight Japan, the United States looked benignly on Mao's movement and urged cooperation of the two groups against Japan.

In the imagery sustained by the Cold War, the Communists are pictured as having always had devious designs for overthrowing established governments and for world conquest. However, during the war and in the early postwar days the Soviet Union and its allied parties around the world played a role of moderation, slowing the pace of revolt. Where Gandhi, for instance, demanded that "Britain quit India," the Indian Communists gave unconditional endorsement to the war effort. American Communists were the most fervid supporters of labor's no-strike pledge, and some suggested that it become a permanent pledge.

There is considerable evidence that Stalin persistently discouraged revolution in Europe, Asia, and Africa. "Near the end of the war," writes historian D. F. Fleming, "Stalin scoffed at Communism in Germany, urged the Italian Reds to make peace with the monarchy, did his best to induce Mao Tse-tung to come to terms with the Kuomintang and angrily demanded of Tito that he back the monarchy, thus fulfilling his [Stalin's] bargain with Churchill." [6] On the morrow of liberation, while De Gaulle was still in Algeria and Italy was in chaos, the Communist-led resistance fighters of France and Italy seized control of the factories. With their large following and their stockpiles of weapons, they could have marched full steam toward political power, or at least attempted it. But General De Gaulle took a plane to Moscow, talked with Stalin, and French Communists thereupon evacuated the factories and dis-

[6] D. F. Fleming, *The Cold War and Its Origins, 1917–1960*, Vol. II, p. 1060.

armed the partisans. Leftist Communists such as Marty and Thillon never forgave Stalin for this. Another word from Moscow and the revolutionary danger abated in Italy—the factories were evacuated, the Garibaldini were relieved of their weapons. So moderate was Communist policy that the French Communists refused to encourage nationalistic movements in the colonies. Uprisings in Madagascar, Algeria, Tunisia, and Morocco occurred despite them, not because of them.

Stalin's moderation, it should be noted, was not the result of any special love for capitalism or for the Western world. Until May 1945, Soviet policy concentrated on assuring complete defeat of Nazi Germany, and Stalin wanted American help in this. French Communist efforts to seize power in France would have endangered the Western Alliance, still vital for victory. Fearful of the atomic bomb, and unable, perhaps unwilling, to support revolutions in other countries, Stalin, although a Marxist, was less a revolutionist than he was a Russian nationalist. In the months after the war, the possibility of American aid for the U.S.S.R. continued to moderate Stalin's West European policies, and the French Communist Party was also restrained by its responsible participation in the new French government.[7]

When the fighting was over, Communists entered "bourgeois governments" eagerly. For almost two years Maurice Thorez was vice-premier of France, and Togliatti held similar status in Italy. Stalin's sights were set on popular fronts with De Gaulle and the Christian Democrats, not revolution.

Here and there Stalin was unable to carry out a pledge. Rather than attempting to establish Communist regimes in Yugoslavia and China, he pressed Tito and Mao Tse-tung to enter coalition regimes. He was rebuffed. He ordered Tito to bring King Peter back to Belgrade but was turned down. As for China, Joseph and Stewart Alsop reported that "Stalin actually did try for a while to keep the promises he gave to Roosevelt at Yalta and to T. V. Soong in Moscow. . . . Stalin ordered Mao Tse-tung and his fellow Chinese Communists to enter a coalition government in China on the terms already laid down by [Patrick] Hurley as President Roosevelt's representative in Chungking. These coalition terms were calculated, or so Hurley believed, to insure that the Communist members of the proposed coalition would be controlled by Chiang and the Nationalists. It would seem that the Hurley view was justified. At any

[7] See Alfred J. Rieber, *Stalin and the French Communist Party, 1941–1947*, especially Chaps. V–VIII.

rate, Mao Tse-tung shared it fully. He flatly refused to obey Stalin's command, declaring that his Communists would win all China in the end and refusing to sacrifice the future victory to a subordinate place in any coalition." [8]

Symptomatic of Soviet Communism's moderation were the events in Greece, where British troops reimposed a conservative monarchy and drove the EAM out of Athens. What was notable about the period before the Cold War was not Stalin's belligerence, but his adherence to agreement. Churchill himself alludes to it: "We have been hampered in our protests against elections in Eastern Europe by the fact that, in order to have freedom to save Greece, Eden and I at Moscow in October (1944) recognized that Russia should have a largely preponderant voice in Rumania and Bulgaria while we took the lead in Greece. Stalin adhered very strictly to this understanding during the thirty days' fighting against the Communists and ELAS in the City of Athens, in spite of the fact that all this was most disagreeable to him and those around him." [9] Not one word of criticism was carried in Soviet newspapers against the terror in Greece.

In the two or three years prior to the full outbreak of the Cold War, Stalin's moderation contributed to averting social upheaval in Western Europe. As late as 1947, Europe was distressingly vulnerable to internal revolt. More than half of Britain's factories were out of production after the great snowstorm that winter. No coal was being mined, millions were unemployed and dispirited. Germany was in worse condition with its cities devastated, its currency virtually worthless, and millions of people without homes or jobs. A cigarette in Berlin could buy twice as much on the black market as a worker could earn for a whole day. In that bleak winter, two hundred people froze to death in Berlin; production was one third of what it had been a decade before. Conditions in France were somewhat better, but iron and steel manufacture was off one half from prewar levels. Europe, in the words of John W. Spanier, political scientist at the University of Florida, was "on the verge of collapse."

Despite this, the West European Communists worked to revive capitalism, not to impose Communism. Joseph Alsop, writing in the New York *Herald Tribune,* July 1946, was struck by the cooperation Jean Monnet was receiving from the Communists in re-

[8] Joseph and Stewart Alsop, New York *Herald Tribune,* July 23, 1951.
[9] Winston Churchill, quoted in D. F. Fleming, *The Cold War and Its Origins, 1917–1960,* Vol. I, p. 182.

building the country. "The key to the success of this plan to date, which has been considerable, is the enthusiastic collaboration of the French Communist Party. . . . Communist leadership has been responsible for such surprising steps as acceptance by the key French unions of a kind of modified piecework system. . . . Reconstruction comes first is the party line." The same collaboration with "bourgeois" governments was taking place in Italy, Belgium, Holland, elsewhere.

The mythology of the Cold War holds that American action "against Communism" was a reaction to the U.S.S.R. (later Chinese) deception. Indeed, in 1948 President Truman charged that the Russians had reneged on thirty-seven pledges, had violated their solemn words at Yalta and Potsdam, had prevented free elections in Poland and Eastern Europe, engineered a *coup d'état* against the coalition regime of Czechoslovakia, carved out an East German state to thwart German unification. These charges were not without some basis in fact, but they ignore many factors that contributed to the hardening of Soviet lines, such as fear of a United States atom-bomb monopoly.[10] Also overlooked is the United States repudiation of portions of the Yalta and other agreements, the agreement as to who should be invited to the San Francisco Conference forming the United Nations, and the guidelines for occupation policy. It is forgotten that the United States had reluctantly agreed to Soviet participation in the occupation of Italy and Japan—agreements that we renegotiated or utilized to exclude a major Soviet role.

The Cold War obviously was the result of factors other than broken treaties. It stemmed in major part from two divergent policies on how the world should be rebuilt in the aftermath of hostilities. One, the long-held strategy of Winston Churchill, held that peace should re-establish the old status quo, or at least as much of it as was viable. This thesis turned its back entirely on Roosevelt's desire for co-existence and, of course, was aimed primarily against nationalist revolution in the colonies and neocolonies.

The other policy was unenunciated but inherent in the burgeoning revolution. Radical nationalism, held in check for a century by imperialism, no longer could be sidetracked. Revolutions were breaking out all over—some five dozen in the ensuing years. The Russians did not initiate them, but once Truman publicly subscribed to the Churchill Doctrine and weakened the wartime alliance, the Soviets attached their tail to the nationalist kite. Only a few of the postwar revolutions were led by outright Communists (China, Indochina),

[10] See Gar Alperovitz, *Atomic Diplomacy: Hiroshima and Potsdam.*

but the salient characteristic of anti-Communism has been that while the United States, reversing the Roosevelt policy, drew apart from the revolution of rising expectations, the Communists attached themselves to it. The United States and its allies did not fight every revolution in every place. It did grant independence to the Philippines (though imposing many conditions that strongly favored American business interests and adversely affected Filipinos); at a certain stage it helped Indonesia achieve independence; it supported Titoist Communism against Stalinist Communism; it came to terms with a number of neutralist countries. But over-all its policy of anti-Communism has been a policy of antirevolution.

III

Ominous signs of divergent attitudes toward the revolution of rising expectations appeared early. After the fall of Mussolini in July 1943, the British restored a discredited monarchy. Reforms were held in abeyance, resistance fighters were disarmed. Even Washington was alarmed in November 1944, when Churchill tried to exclude Count Sforza, the liberal leader of the Committee of National Liberation, from the Italian government. In Belgium and Greece, Britain similarly revived conservative monarchies.

While the commitment to conservative governments remained the bulwark of Churchill's policy toward Europe, it represented the salient factor of his overriding imperial concern to preserve the British empire. This commitment was dramatized in developments in Madagascar, a remote island in the Indian Ocean that belonged to France. At the outset of hostilities it had been occupied by Britain to prevent it from falling into the hands of either the Nazis or Vichy France. In 1943, by agreement with De Gaulle, the British turned the colony back to Free French troops. The Malagasy leaders, mindful of the promises of the Atlantic Charter, asked for the right of self-government.

De Gaulle offered them instead a devious plan by which Madagascar would be part of a French Union with its foreign affairs, internal security, and so forth, controlled by the French. According to this plan, the four million Malagasy would be represented in the French parliament by three delegates, and the fifty thousand French colonists by a similar number. The native delegates arrived in Paris, denounced the scheme as a sham, and refused to take their seats. Meanwhile, the Malagasy people had attacked a military camp at Houramanja, and fighting had erupted. When the clouds had lifted the three members of parliament were in jail, sentenced to death (later commuted to life imprisonment on the Comores Islands). Thousands were arrested, and, by official count, eighty thousand Malagasy and two hundred French were killed. The nationalist council claimed 220,000 deaths. Some were thrown from airplanes; some were buried alive.

Similar outbursts occurred in Algeria, Tunisia, and Morocco, for the same reasons and with the same results. The natives demanded independence and De Gaulle, with the assent of Churchill, answered with machine-gun fire. Forty-five thousand Moslems died in Algeria in 1945, seven thousand in Tunisia.

The first spurt of revolutionary effort failed. Others did not. Nationalism succeeded in planting its flag peacefully in many states— India, Ceylon, Pakistan, Burma, the old French territories in Africa, Tanganyika, Sudan, Uganda—but almost always one step ahead of the sheriff. India achieved independence from a greatly enervated Britain in 1947, then under a Labour government, following a wave of strikes in 1945–46 and revolts in the Indian Army and Air Force. Tanganyika and Uganda were freed in the wake of the so-called Mau Mau rebellion in the third section of East Africa, Kenya. France yielded her colonies in Africa only after being defeated in Indochina and being confronted by guerrilla war in Algeria. It cannot be said, therefore, that the West withdrew to honor the pledges of the Atlantic Charter but, in most instances, because it became unfeasible or too costly to hold on.

In other places, national revolutions were accompanied by violence as the West tried to re-establish colonial rule. The lessons of Indonesia, Indochina, and Korea are particularly instructive in this respect.

Early in World War II Japan seized the complex of thousands of islands called Indonesia (Dutch East Indies) and held it until August 1945. Five times nationalist movements organized revolts against the occupying power, but in vain. Two days after the Japanese surrender, the Indonesian nationalists, led by Achmed Sukarno and Mohammed Hatta, issued a declaration of independence reminiscent of the one drafted by Jefferson in 1776. The matter should have ended here, for there is no question that Sukarno and Hatta had the allegiance of the mass of Indonesians.

But six weeks later British troops arrived from India and paved the way for the return of Dr. Hubertus J. van Mook as governor general for the Dutch, and thousands of Dutch troops. The Dutch even used the Japanese Kempeitai (secret police) to "restore order" until they could build up their own military forces. General Douglas MacArthur, commenting in Tokyo on the use of Japanese troops, passionately exclaimed: "If there is anything that makes my blood boil it is to see our allies in Indochina and Java deploying Japanese troops to reconquer the little people we promised to liberate. It is the most ignoble kind of betrayal." [11] Nevertheless, American military aid to the Netherlands continued, and Indonesian leaders, patiently waiting to have their independence ratified, complained to the United States that vehicles carrying American markings were shooting at them. Washington, in response, asked the Dutch to remove the American markings.

Amsterdam recognized the de facto authority of the Republic of Indonesia in Java, Sumatra, and Madura, and agreed to relinquish the rest by January 1949, providing the Indonesian leaders agreed to become part of a Netherlands-Indonesian Union, under a common queen, and to restore Dutch property.

The Dutch, however, were merely sparring for time. Van Mook later admitted his country intended to hold on to the lush colony for at least fifteen or twenty years more. The Dutch General S. H. Spoor told *The New York Times,* on February 14, 1947, that "the policy I will follow is that of the late President Theodore Roosevelt; namely, soft words backed up by a big stick." [12] In May 1947, when the Dutch build-up had reached eleven thousand soldiers, they struck. The United Nations and an aroused United States came to the support of the nationalists—at least verbally—but in December 1948 the Dutch parachutists descended on Jakarta, arrested Sukarno, Hatta, and others, and virtually restored Indonesia to colonial status.

Fortunately, the United Nations and the United States came to the aid of the nationalists, and after uprisings that in four and a half years claimed a hundred thousand lives, Indonesia became independent in 1950. One of the factors that undoubtedly contributed to Washington's response on behalf of the nationalists was an abortive 1948 uprising against the republic by the Communists in the Madium area. The republicans, said the Communists, were compromising with the imperialists. Washington felt that the support of the more moderate nationalists would keep the Communists at bay.

The pattern here, however, is quite interesting. The colonial

[11] Edgar Snow, *The Other Side of the River: Red China Today,* p. 686.
[12] David Anderson, dispatch from The Hague, *The New York Times,* February 14, 1947.

powers would rhetorically agree to independence, then bring back
their troops, build them up (with the aid of Britain and the United
States), and try to smash the revolution.

The formula in Indochina, where the Vietnam War now rages, is
similar. During the war two groups contested the Japanese: the
Vietminh (National Front), made up of many groups including
the Communists, and the Dong Minh Hoi, which played a lesser
role. The U.S. Office of Strategic Services (OSS) helped the Vietminh when ten thousand of its guerrillas were fighting the Japanese.
The Vietminh liberated its northern provinces and established a
broad national government, supported even by Chiang Kai-shek. On
March 6, 1946, France itself recognized the regime of a "free state
with its own government, parliament, army and finances, forming
part of the Indochinese Federation of the French Union."

Though Roosevelt had promised before his death that no French
soldier would ever be permitted to set foot on Indochinese soil
again, the British opened the door to De Gaulle's forces. With military power at their command the French, like the Dutch in Indonesia, stiffened their posture. They insisted on dividing the territory
into a number of sections, with the South to have its own administration. In four months of negotiations with Ho, France refused to
give up control over the army, foreign affairs, currency, and the
economy. Union as the Vietminh saw it was simply a figleaf for
continued colonialism. Incidents flared. On November 23, 1946, a
French cruiser fired on the Vietnamese section of Haiphong. Six
thousand were killed, guerrilla war broke out and lasted for eight
long years until in 1954 the guerrilla force under General Giap
(with 70,000 men) defeated the French (with 166,000 troops).

Despite Roosevelt's promises of self-determination, Truman and
Eisenhower, with the Cold War intensified, gave between $2 billion
and $3 billion in aid to the French from 1950 to 1954 to help sup-
press the Vietminh. Late in 1952, Americans in Saigon boasted
that the two hundredth ship with supplies for the French had been
unloaded. At the time France was defeated, John Foster Dulles was
urging her to persevere and was trying to forge an alliance of
Britain, France, and the United States to continue the war. According to Roscoe Drummond and Gaston Coblentz, in their book *Duel
at the Brink,* Dulles went so far as to offer the French three atom
bombs to be used at Dienbienphu and the Chinese border. Under
the banner of anti-Communism, the United States was helping
throttle the nationalist revolution.

The postwar history of Korea reveals how the fear of nationalist

revolution drives American policy into an alliance with conservatives that in the end aids Communism. Here, as World War II
ended, the resistance movement that had fought Japan for decades
held an assembly two days before General John R. Hodge landed
with his occupying force. A nationalist government was formed
much as had happened in Indonesia and Indochina. Some of the
leaders were Communists, and other revolutionary committees were
headed by non-Communists, such as the one in the province of
Cholla Nam Do, where a pro-American group led by a Christian
pastor was in the saddle.

Hodge, however, refused to recognize the People's Republic government which would have ruled for *all* Korea. Instead, so certain
was he that the United States and Communism were on a collision
course, he chose to govern the southern half of the country Syngman Rhee, a returned exile of conservative mien, aligned with the
landowners. Rhee's power was based not on a national army but on
a constabulary whose key elements were the same police who had
served under Japan. Since Russia would not accept Rhee, Hodge
would not accept the northern leftists, and there were soon two
Koreas with the makings of war. In the North the Soviets did use
the revolutionary committees as the kernel of their regime, and of
course with that kind of support the Communists became predominant. (It is worth noting, by contrast, that when the United States
and the Soviets agreed to a unified Austria, a permanent non-Communist regime emerged and still operates. Had it remained divided
there would have been, as in Korea and Germany, a Communist
regime in one part and an anti-Communist one in the other.)

IV

Anti-Communism's worst postwar defeat was in China. No victory of American foreign policy since remotely compensates for this
setback. Mao Tse-tung's ascent to power in a nation with one
quarter of the world's population ranks in historic importance with
the Russian and French Revolutions. The tragic fact is that anti-
Communism itself contributed more than a little to Communism's
success in 1949. As in Russia in 1917, the evidence is overwhelming that the West's failure to join hands with revolutionary aspirations drove nationalist elements toward the alternative shelter of
Communism.

Western relations with China is an ugly story beginning with the
Opium War of 1839–42: China was forced to cede Hong Kong to

the British along with five other ports for trade and residence; the Taiping Rebellion, 1850–64, which would have created a true national state in China, was suppressed; the Boxers were attacked militarily; China was divided into all kinds of spheres of influence for the great powers; and key economic ports were seized for foreigners. In addition to these affronts, Japan seized Korea and Formosa.

In 1911, six years before the Bolshevik Revolution, a physician named Sun Yat-sen led a revolt against the decadent Manchu dynasty. As with the Mexican Revolution the year before, Sun and his nationalists were unable immediately to unify the country, evict the foreigners, or change the feudal land system. For fifteen years the Chinese Revolution and the Kuomintang had to contend with war lords and the world powers who supported them. Meanwhile Japan, abetted and recognized by the other powers, including the United States, continued to carve away pieces of the nation. The Versailles Treaty legalized conquests in Manchuria, Inner Mongolia, and Port Arthur.

But if the West would not come to the aid of Sun, the Russian Bolsheviks would and did. Sun had no place else to go. Bolshevik technicians, therefore, were welcomed to build a revolutionary army, form unions, organize peasant and student groups. With Communist talent and skills the Kuomintang by 1925–27 was able to unify the country under its tutelage.

Sun Yat-sen died in 1925, his work left in mid-air. His place was taken by his brother-in-law, Chiang Kai-shek, who on his own or through foreign inducement—we can't say which—was turning severely to the right. Chiang sundered the coalition and, on achieving victory, turned on his Communist allies and massacred them. Instead of instituting reforms, especially land reform, he kept and strengthened the status quo. Aligned with Britain, France, and the United States, Chiang's people, as Graham Peck writes, "became cheats and murderers. . . . The way they came to power determined the personnel, techniques, direction, and final destination of their government." [13]

The West still had an opportunity to pressure Chiang for major changes to make nationalism and reform on behalf of people's welfare meaningful; but it didn't. Nor did it interfere, after 1931, when Japan moved deeper into Manchuria—though the United States criticized the conquest. (Contrast this, however, with American intervention in Vietnam, Cuba, the Dominican Republic, Iran,

[13] Graham Peck, *Two Kinds of Time*, p. 69.

and Guatemala *against* Communists and nationalists.) For the rest, nothing changed. The cry of the peasant for land remained unappeased. Corruption was rampant.

This was the prelude to the Communist victory of 1946–49. It followed Western indifference—hostility would be more correct— to nationalist revolution. In China, as in Russia in 1917 and Cuba in 1960, the Communists were beneficiaries of a revolution that they did not start but to which they attached themselves. When Chiang, abetted by the West, aborted the revolutionary nationalist urge brought into focus by Sun Yat-sen, tens of thousands of soldiers, literati, intellectuals, socialists joined the Communists to complete Sun Yat-sen's revolution. (The same thing happened, and is happening, in Vietnam, where Buddhists and other nationalists have joined the National Liberation Front because they can see no other alternative.)

Mao's victory in 1949 was not the result of superior military power; on the contrary, he was far inferior in that department. Where Chiang received $3 billion in aid from the United States, Mao received a relatively small number of weapons which the Russians had seized on entering Manchuria. The Kuomintang reportedly had four million men under arms in addition to modern weapons, but in just seventeen months of combat, from July 1946 to November 1947, it lost almost half. Mountains of American weapons fell into Maoist hands, and some were sold by corrupt Kuomintang leaders—just as in Vietnam in more recent years. One could make a good case for the contention that American supplies to Chiang helped the Communists as much as they helped Chiang.

The Kuomintang had been defeated militarily, true; but when it lost the loyalties of the intelligentsia and the little people of the towns, and when the agricultural countryside rose in revolt against long neglect and oppression, it was then that the Kuomintang finally lost the nation.

Decisive for the Maoists' victory was a superior social approach, an emphasis on a nationalism bent on reform. Whether Mao, in power, adhered to his avowed principles or not is beside the point. During the revolution he galvanized millions of intellectuals and peasants who literally were without any other real choice. The vacuum created by Chiang and his Western allies was filled by Mao and his nationalist allies, who captured the nationalist sentiment of China.

It wasn't that the United States opposed reform. In a section of the U.S. State Department's China White Paper, 1949, devoted to "American Efforts to Encourage Reform of the Chinese Government," can be read Ambassador to China John Leighton Stuart's testimony to this fact. "Dr. Stuart said that he had many times outlined to the Generalissimo [Chiang Kai-shek] the type of adjustments which were considered prerequisites to a more positive policy and assistance on the part of the U.S. He said that the type of change which he had in mind centered around basic reform through constitutional institutions within the body of the Government, including the delegation of more authority, the establishment and visible maintenance and protection of civil liberties, and the actual development of a more intimate working relationship between the Government and the people. . . . The Ambassador again emphasized the need for drastic overall reform." [14]

Periodically, Roosevelt and General Marshall, as Truman's emissary, pleaded with Chiang to make changes—just as Eisenhower, Kennedy, and Johnson pleaded with Diem and Ky in Vietnam—but the policy of anti-Communism drove the United States into consort with reaction. When a choice had to be made, the United States had no allies but the conservatives. Political leaders in China told Professor Nathaniel Peffer of Columbia University in May 1947 that there was no need to institute reforms because America was destined to war with Russia and would have to support them anyway.

The doctrine of anti-Communism in the period following World War II, as in the period following World War I, conceives of Communism as a major enemy, not because it is totalitarian or dictatorial, but because it challenges the status quo. Although the U.S. has only once since World War II mustered a show of force against a rightist regime (in the Dominican Republic after the fall of Trujillo), it has refused consistently to take even strong economic measures against the 1967 military dictatorship in Greece, the apartheidist regime in South Africa, the fascist regime in Spain (which hasn't held a free election in its whole history since 1936), the Portuguese government of Salazar, the Castelo Branco and Costa e Silva military rule in Brazil, the Somoza dictatorship in Nicaragua, and on and on. Truman, in speaking of his Truman Doctrine, once equated "freedom" with "free enterprise." Communism, on the other hand, has offered a haven for nations and leaders who seek to upset the world-wide system of colonialism and neocolonialism based on free enterprise.

[14] *United States Relations with China,* Department of State Publication 3573, Far Eastern Series 30, released August 1949, p. 252.

The anti-Communist policy has actually been aimed at a much wider spectrum than the Communists. To sustain as much of the old order as is sustainable, the U.S. has supported conservative elements who opposed even non-Communist nationalism. The CIA in the 1950's helped overthrow the governments of Mossadegh in Iran and Arbenz in Guatemala. Both were non-Communists, both were replaced by men far to the right. Washington intervened with twenty-seven thousand soldiers and Marines against a revolution on April 28, 1965, in the Dominican Republic aimed at restoring to power a constitutionally elected non-Communist President, Juan Bosch. The U.S. applauded the ouster of Joao Goulart, a neutralist and non-Communist in Brazil in April 1964 and gave enthusiastic support to the military regime of Castelo Branco and Costa e Silva that replaced it. The State Department has rejoiced at the ouster of non-Communists such as Nkrumah of Ghana or Sukarno of Indonesia.

Anti-Communism in the Western Hemisphere manifests the same goals and methods as in Africa and Asia. In Cuba, the United States twice helped a reactionary militarist, Batista, seize and stay in power (in the 1930's and 1950's) without anything resembling democracy or democratic elections. But when a genuine, originally non-Communist nationalist, Fidel Castro, led a band of twelve hundred guerrillas and mobilized the whole nation to force Batista to flee, Washington was unable to come to an understanding with him. Castro's threat to nationalize American sugar holdings and distribute them to peasants, as part of an agrarian reform, met unabashed hostility and led ultimately not only to a diplomatic break, but to the American-sponsored Bay of Pigs invasion by Cuban exiles. Castro, a non-Communist who received no support from the Communists until a few months before he came to power, turned to the Soviet orbit for help and to Communism for an ideology. There is still a considerable amount of emotion surrounding American attitudes toward Castro, but there is little doubt that in this instance the policy of anti-Communism actually created a Communist state.

A similar predilection toward the right and the militarists was evidenced in Bolivia in 1964. A genuine nationalist revolution broke out in that country in 1952, uprooting the old military caste and substituting for it a workers' and peasants' militia, plus a small standing army. Communists and Trotskyists, never in power, nonetheless had strong bases in the unions and other movements. The leading figures of the center, President Paz Estenssoro, was in constant strife with the leftists, but he did not liquidate the militia system. The United States, on the other hand, constantly pressed him—and other presidents—to change over to a traditional army. When Paz found himself in difficulties within his party, beleaguered from right and left, he acceded to the American suggestion, enlarged his standing army from four thousand to twenty thousand—and soon after, in 1964, was overthrown by a friend of American General Curtis LeMay, General Rene Barrientos. How much collusion there was between the American military, the CIA and Barrientos is not known, but his regime, as expected, has turned right of center and is now challenged by leftist guerrillas in the hills.

CONCLUSION

Anti-Communism—antirevolution—in foreign affairs inevitably has had a backlash in internal American politics, a backlash that will be reviewed later.

In 1788, Alexander Hamilton warned about overemphasizing security. "To be more safe," he wrote, "the nations at length become willing to run the risk of being less free." [15] Anti-Communism today places us precisely in this position—less free. More importantly, the obsession with anti-Communism has prevented the United States from understanding the forces of revolution or disruptive change. The history of anti-Communism reveals a reflex response, an effort to confront and not accommodate, and an emotional refusal to empathize with or respond to demands for an improved life on the part of the emerging nation.

[15] Alexander Hamilton, quoted in Walter Millis, "How to Compete with the Russians," *The New York Times Magazine,* February 2, 1958.

2. WHAT IS IT?: The Anti-Communism Complex

ANTI-COMMUNISM has deep, indigenous roots among our people. The rapid expansion of our country, although it developed what is probably a unique openness and friendliness in the American character, carried with it also a suspicion of the stranger in town and the consequent compulsion on the part of the stranger to identify himself as a good American. A still more effective factor is our heterogeneity: We Americans are all immigrants. We are all hyphenated Americans. None of us belongs in the sense of the European whose ancestry in his own land and in his own local community goes back a thousand years. We have not been born into our acceptability; we have had to prove it. We have had to demonstrate to one another that we are good Americans—primarily by demonstrating that we are not un-American. One of the authors of this study asked a Danish Communist, Professor Mogens Fog, who *as a Communist* had served as a minister of his government, "Which are you first—a Communist or a Dane?" Professor Fog replied, "Only an American could ask such a question. Every Dane is as much a Dane as every other."

A similar attitude was taken by Winston Churchill in the House of Commons when he resisted pressure to declare the Communist Party illegal since it was opposed to the war. Churchill said that the English Communist Party was composed of Englishmen, and he did not fear an Englishman—something, a social scientist has observed, "that an American leader could not say." [1]

An Un-Danish (or Un-British or Un-French) Activities Committee is unthinkable. Oaths of nondisloyalty (which any traitor would gladly take) are likewise unknown outside of dictatorships. But such fantastic concepts and procedures are easily generated in a populace composed, like ours, of people who left foreign lands (or whose near ancestors did) and brought to the New World with them suspicious—that is, strange—manners, customs, languages, and (who could say?) ideas. Side by side with the flourishing of our free institutions this susceptibility to suspicion abides.

Anti-Communism in the United States represents such a dynamic

---

[1] Seymour Martin Lipset in Daniel Bell (ed.), *The Radical Right,* p. 267.

complex, a complex that has grown from the impact of history on the anxieties and hopes of the American people, and has achieved such psychological and political structure as to have a life of its own.

A great deal of anti-Communism is basically a reaction to an America caught up in the throes of change. It is fear, not only of Communism but of change, a fear which is prone to confuse the two; a fear fed by the changing character of American life.

In the United States, social positions that were regarded as central to the American way of life were rapidly disestablished. The corner grocery yielded to the supermarket, usually managed by great holding companies. The small farm rapidly lost ground to the more efficient and highly capitalized industrial farm. The medical profession sank perceptibly in relative status as more and more educated citizens took their place in society and even displayed the title of Doctor. Town fathers across the country had to yield place to new kinds of active citizens, often from out of town. City bosses found their bailiwicks threatened by reform movements. Working-class whites in the South and in the industrial North found themselves competing with hitherto subservient Negro citizens. Self-made men of great wealth were disturbed by the rise of sophisticated and specially educated corporate managers. In short, large numbers of American citizens rather suddenly found their status undermined and their expectations frustrated. They were ready to be angry at any identifiable cause.

Thus social turmoil has eroded traditional social positions and displaced power. There has been a weakening of the relationship between class position and power; political power rather than wealth has become decisive; education rather than property has become the source of power. "Social groups that are dispossessed invariably seek targets on which they can vent their resentments, targets whose power can serve to explain their disposition." [2] Communism becomes for them a convenient scapegoat.

There are many who are susceptible to this explanation for their social anxiety over the complexity of life in the United States in the twentieth century. There are small businessmen who have acquired wealth which has not brought with it status or power in decision-making. There are third- and fourth-generation immigrants who have succeeded materially but whose wealth has not won them social acceptance into the mainstream of American life. Thus, Joseph Kennedy, rankled that Boston newspapers always referred

[2] Daniel Bell, ibid., p. 3.

to him as Irish, said once, "I was born here, my children were born here. What the hell do I have to do to be an American?" [3] It has been noted that Senator Joseph McCarthy drew a disproportionate amount of support from Catholics of recent immigrant background. Perhaps these people felt that if they proved their patriotism by hating Communism, they would be accepted.

There are men of great wealth who see an increasingly centralized government curbing their activities, regulating their business ventures, taxing their finances. They equate Communism with liberal social legislation that would redistribute wealth. "I equate the welfare state with Socialism and Socialism with Communism," says Dan Smoot, a former FBI agent whose extensive radio and television programs are financed with Texas oil money.[4] Along with their finances, prosperous men often accumulate anxieties about their ability to preserve what they have acquired. They fear that forces are afoot to deprive them of their gain, and they find in anti-Communism a welcome outlet for their fear.

A further group who find anti-Communism appealing is the religious fundamentalists. They too live in a changing world whose changes have threatened them. A liberal interpretation of scripture has won the day and the major Protestant denominations have embraced it. Only the fundamentalists fight a rear-guard action for the "true faith." And "they have found a fighting issue that helps them to surmount their previous isolation, an issue on which at last they have common ground with all America: they are implacably and consumingly anti-Communist, and in the grand ecumenism of their anti-Communist passion they welcome all allies." [5]

So via television channels, over the radio waves, at church meetings, and at community anti-Communist schools those who have been termed "the Christian fright peddlers" [6] assail the internal and external threat of Communism. They are religious leaders in the holy crusade that finds in Communism the modern equivalent of the devil. And as Richard Hofstadter has observed, "Many preachers have discovered that they can arouse more fervor and raise more cash by politicising their message than they can by appealing solely to the religious sensibilities of the audience." [7] Vast sums of money have been poured into the coffers of these evangelical protesters

---

[3] Quoted by Seymour Martin Lipset, *ibid.*, p. 280.
[4] Quoted by Daniel Bell, *ibid.*, p. 12.
[5] Richard Hofstadter, *The Paranoid Style in American Politics*, p. 80.
[6] *The Christian Fright Peddlers*, Brooks R. Walker, Doubleday (1964).
[7] Hofstadter, *The Paranoid Style in American Politics*, p. 73.

against political, social, and religious changes that they deplore and brand "Communistic."

Another class of citizen who finds anti-Communism a convenient instrument is government leaders. It is difficult to probe behind the rhetoric to the convictions that may lie behind it. Politicians who run for public office are mindful of the importance of taking a public posture against all things "Communistic." Especially those who are liberal may find it necessary to convince suspicious voters that on the issue of Communism they are clean.

Since World War II, administration after administration has taken an anti-Communist position as the Cold War has dominated the international scene. Legislation that might otherwise have occasioned serious debate has been passed with the assurance that it would somehow help counter Communism. Thus vast defense appropriations are voted, loyalty probes initiated, internal security measures approved, and a disastrous war undertaken in Southeast Asia, and all are rationalized as part of a never-ending campaign to keep Communism under control.

There can be little doubt that government officials raise the spectre of Communism to justify a policy which may be insupportable on other grounds. So when a critic of the war in Vietnam questioned whether the war really is in America's self-interest, Secretary of State Rusk pointed to the hundreds of millions of Chinese Communists just beyond North Vietnam's border. The implication was clear: The war in Vietnam had to be seen in a larger perspective; the problem was not simply Vietnam but Communist China.

The United States faces a complex world in the 1960's, a world in which for all its power it cannot impose its own patterns for development. It is a world without the tidy colonial systems managed by major powers. It is a world where Russia is for the first time an international force to be reckoned with, a world in which a growing China stands in the wings. It is a world where the underprivileged are rising to demand freedom from the deprivations they have known in the past. Confronted with such a world, frustrated by their inability to manage these forces, America's leaders too are tempted to use the machinations of Communism as the explanation for their own dilemmas.

Although there are identifiable social groups in the United States in which anti-Communism is strong, it would be a serious mistake to conclude that the attitude is restricted to these groups. Anti-Communism pervades our entire society. It is not argued. It is an

unchallenged American assumption that Communism is bad, and
from this logically follows the belief that whatever is against Communism is good. Add to this the disturbing observation of an
American sociologist that "basically there is some undefined segment of the population that responds to the need to hate." [8]

It may be that Communism provides a convenient target upon
which Americans find release for their pent-up hostilities, and it
may be that Americans find in Communism a handy way to explain
a troublesome world. There are no doubt manifold reasons for this
phenomenon. Yet the fact remains, anti-Communism is woven into
the fabric of American society. It wins votes, it sells weapons, it
guides policy makers, it excites legislators. Modern America is not
understandable unless one realizes that a fear, a hatred, an obsession
with Communism has helped mold our country into what it has
become in the twentieth century.

Anti-Communism is essentially negative in its political quality;
it is based on fear and a sense of threat to the nation and to valued
qualities of life. The threat is perceived as emanating from a
powerful, pervasive, and mysterious force. "Communism," that is,
the image of this force in the American political mind, means
different things to different people and many things to most people;
but, above all, it represents danger to the nation.

The popular American image of Communism has been built
from many elements over a considerable period of time. As with
all stereotype images, most of the components of the anti-Communist perception of Communism are based on kernels of fact;
for example, Communist theory predicts social revolution and
Communist political practice involves efforts to foment such revolution. But it does not follow that every major social change, even
in the direction predicted by the Communist idea, is the result of
Communist forces at work. Anti-Communism has the power to
deceive us about our problems, for it seems to persuade us that
they can be solved by the easy operation of delivering a culprit or
band of culprits into our loyal hands. From the post-Revolutionary
Alien and Sedition Acts (when our new republic was in danger of
war with France) down to our own time, in which Secretary
General U Thant of the United Nations pleads with us to see the
fighting in Vietnam not as "an anti-Communist holy war" but as
a struggle for national independence, we have been prone to accept
the easy solution to our problems: They are caused by agitators
and plotters and traitors and conspirators.

[8] Seymour Martin Lipset in Daniel Bell (ed.), *The Radical Right*, p. 366.

Let us identify first some of the principal elements in the anti-Communist's image of Communism and then the anti-Communist's image of himself and his world.

THE ANTI-COMMUNIST'S VIEW OF COMMUNISM

1. *Radical Revolution.* "Workers of the world unite—you have nothing to lose but your chains." Communism has been a revolutionary force that has caused considerable dislocation and turmoil as it transformed society. Communism certainly aims at the radical reorganization of society. From this fact the anti-Communist concludes that all manner of social legislation is movement in the direction of the ultimate disastrous transposition of society. Reform is really revolution in disguise and creeping socialism unchecked becomes Communism at full gallop. So reasons the anti-Communist.

2. *Monolithic Conspiracy.* Periodically in Russia, international meetings are held to decide Communist policy. The anti-Communist concludes that these members of the Party in various nations then carry out the policy unhesitatingly. The Communists are extremely well organized and their decisions are synchronized by the Party mechanism operating through Moscow. Party leaders in the Muscovite capital snap their fingers and the Party partisans everywhere jump. So reasons the anti-Communist.

3. *Dictatorialness.* A Communist government indeed seeks to impose its will upon the people. From this the anti-Communist concludes that everything that is not mandatory is forbidden in a Communist country. The people have no choice in the condition of their life. They fulfill the government's dictates or they suffer dire consequences. Such governments are by nature unpopular. So reasons the anti-Communist.

4. *Expansionism.* Proclamations of the International Communist movement characteristically predict world revolution eventuating in a Communist world. From this the anti-Communist concludes that revolutions are packaged in Moscow and Peking and exported around the world. Now they have devised a devilishly clever doctrine: "wars of national liberation." They practice what Marvin E. Gettleman has caricatured as "the push-button theory of insurrection (the button is pushed in some outside place, and immediately 'infiltrators' come pouring out of a cornucopia and guerrillas are activated)." [9] We have seen China fall under the control of Com-

----

[9] *The Progressive,* August 1967, in a review of *The First Vietnamese Crisis* by Melvin Gurtov.

munism, and Cuba, and the Eastern European countries. Where
will it end? Unless it is stopped, the United States will be the next.
So reasons the anti-Communist.

5. *Godlessness*. The Communists are atheists. From this the
anti-Communist concludes that Communists are morally inferior
human beings. Since God embraces all that is good, godlessness
(Communism) must be the summation of all that is evil. The proponents of atheistic Communism are tainted with the dye of their
wicked doctrines.

The anti-Communist feels that advocates of social reform are
Communists, and the religious fundamentalist is persuaded that
liberal religious leaders, urging the social application of faith, have
fallen under the sway of Communism. A new dimension is added
to the fundamentalistic attack on liberal religion. Communism is
the Devil Incarnate and the undermining of the old-time religion
becomes one of his obvious and vicious works. So reasons the anti-
Communist.

6. *Deceitfulness*. Communists have been dishonest on many occasions. The anti-Communist concludes there is no use in negotiat-
ing with the Communists—inasmuch as they will honor treaties
only insofar as it is convenient to their purpose to do so. They are,
in J. Edgar Hoover's phrase, "masters of deceit." Their complete
lack of integrity renders diplomatic dealing with them not only
hazardous but futile, for they can't be counted on to live up to their
end of an agreement. So reasons the anti-Communist.

7. *Subhuman and Superhuman Character*. Communists have
been cruel and they have been clever. Contradictory though it may
appear, in the mind of the anti-Communist, the Communist is accredited with both subhuman limitations and superhuman powers.
He lacks the human emotions of compassion, tenderness, and hu-
mor on the one hand, and, on the other, he is endowed with incredible abilities that enable him to snare other people into furthering his purposes. They steal for him, they spy for him, they serve
as his dupes, masking his diabolical plotting with the cloak of respectability. So reasons the anti-Communist.

8. *Conspiracy and Subversion*. Communists have conspired to
undermine and topple established governments. The anti-Communist concludes that unwanted historical events are the outcome
of sinister machinations by a handful of evil men. They managed to
steal our atomic secrets. China was lost to the Communists because
Owen Lattimore plotted from a desk in the State Department. In
the 1950's Senator Joseph R. McCarthy said that there were 205

card-carrying Communists in the State Department. Communism now embraces a sizable portion of the globe and in none of the lands where it has come to power did it do so through free elections. Like termites, Communists nibble away at the understructure of a legitimate government until it collapses. They have no understanding of what the democratic political process is, or perhaps they do and know that they could never achieve a political victory by those means. Therefore, they resort to underhanded methods. So reasons the anti-Communist.

9. *Infiltration.* Communists have worked their way into private organizations and taken them over. The anti-Communist concludes they are now in Parent-Teacher Associations, in schools, in churches, and in labor unions. They have infiltrated our colleges and universities; they are at work in peace organizations and civil rights groups. In the peace demonstrations and racial disturbances, even in the hippie movement, in this country one finds examples of their effectiveness. The Right Reverend John Pickney, Episcopal Bishop of Upper South Carolina, saw the devastating riots of the summer of 1967 as "part of a Communist plot to take over the world." Looking for his runaway daughter, the minister of a large San Francisco church roamed that city's Haight-Ashbury district in disguise. He ingratiated himself with the young hippies, telling them that "the church has not met the needs of our age"; but when his identity was made known, he informed the San Francisco *Chronicle* that "privately he does not hold that opinion and believes the Communists are behind the hippie movement." So reasons the anti-Communist.

THE ANTI-COMMUNIST'S VIEW OF HIMSELF

1. *Assumption of United States Superiority.* "We would never stoop to the practices of the Communists." The United States is a God-fearing nation. We have a divine mission to uphold the principles of righteousness, justice, and peace. Honesty characterizes our dealings. This nation, under God, provides a luminous example of rectitude for the rest of the world to follow.

We are a peace-loving nation. Whenever we go to war, it is always for the sake of others. We joined in World War I to make the world safe for democracy. We entered World War II to save the world from the scourge of Hitlerism. And we are in Vietnam to save a little nation from being ravaged by Communist aggression.

We are a generous nation. We have given away billions of dollars in recent decades to help the poor of the world. History will record the United States to be the most philanthropic country that ever existed. We have fed multitudes of people with millions of tons of surplus foods. We have bestowed technical aid on many nations. We have played the world's rich uncle, spreading our beneficences around the globe.

We are a freedom-loving people. Other governments are inclined to repression or are careless about the civil liberties of their citizens, but our land was conceived in liberty and born in liberating strife. We were determined to be free from England's rule and want other people to be free to decide their own destinies too. That is why we are at war in Vietnam. That is the reason we go to war and fight for freedom. We no longer have a War Department in our government; we have a Defense Department, and go to war only in defense of freedom.

We are a model nation. Any country that wants to amount to something can fashion itself after the American paragon. After all, we are the richest and most powerful country in the world, aren't we? If other countries want wealth and power, let them follow our example.

It is important to understand what we are trying to do in the world. We are simply trying to help people who can't help themselves. Most other countries in the world are underdeveloped, lacking American intelligence, American know-how, American political skills and acumen. So, out of the goodness of our hearts, we are trying to help them catch up with us. We have no aim in view but to lift the world's people to a higher standard of living and protect them from the theft of their liberties by Communism.

Unfortunately, many in the world do not understand us. They misunderstand our motives and, lacking American insight, they are not so deeply aware of the Communist menace. They are consequently not duly appreciative of our labors on their behalf. They are not properly grateful for all we have done for them. The world has been spoiled by American benevolence. Many have come to look upon American largess as their right. So reasons the anti-Communist.

2. *Western Superiority.* "We belong to the Free World." The Communists and their satellites are that part of the world that has been deprived of freedom. In contrast, the Western world is composed of those people who still have their freedom. The Free World is also the Christian World that has been informed and nurtured by the faith. It is that portion of the globe that is dedicated

to the preservation of Christian values. So it was that Winston Churchill on March 5, 1946, in Fulton, Missouri, called upon the English-speaking peoples to "lead 'Christian' civilization in an anti-Communist crusade." The non-Communist world represents Christian civilization, and its superiority to the rest of the world should be obvious to every thinking man. So reasons the anti-Communist.

DYNAMICS OF THE ANTI-COMMUNIST COMPLEX

The principal elements of the psychopolitical viewpoint of anti-Communism—perceptions of Communist revolutionism, atheism, expansionism, and subversion—reinforce one another in complimentary ways. Communism, to the individual anti-Communist, is apprehended as a whole, every aspect of which is evil and threatening. The over-all effect within the body politic is also greater than the sum of component reactions. Diverse motives activate different elements of the society to the same common end; persons suffering status frustration respond to the process of social change, religious fundamentalists to the element of atheism, parochial patriots to international competition, and authoritarian persons to the image of subversion.

In other words, not all anti-Communists show every symptom that comprises the syndrome. Some fear Communism basically for economic reasons. They see its tentacles reaching out to grasp their wealth. Others are motivated primarily by religious considerations, and Communism's attack on religion makes them tremble for their faith. Communism's missionary zeal, its avowed intention to win the world to its ideology, causes the nationalist acute worry about this nation's security.

The anti-Communist complex is a shifting, changing thing. Within it are to be found wide variations in apprehension, strange combinations and overlaps of anxiety. As has been noted, in recent years there has been a relaxing of the anti-Communist attitude toward the Soviet Union, but the irrational emotion once aroused by this land has been transferred to China. Peking is now capable of arousing an antipathy formerly reserved for Moscow.

It is interesting to speculate on why this shift has occurred. Perhaps there has been grudging though sincere admiration for Soviet space achievement. The brutal excesses of the Stalinist regime have been moderated, and Khrushchev, bucolic and ebullient, was a good public relations man for his nation whether he was standing in an Iowa corn field or conversing with Mrs. John F.

Kennedy. Probably cultural exchanges have helped America see the Soviet Union in a new light, and the visiting ballets and orchestras have tempered American public opinion. In the meanwhile Communist China remains far away, unknown, inscrutable—and sinister.

It is not the contention of this essay that Communism contains no disagreeable elements, for there are aspects of Communism that are a legitimate cause of concern. But it is our contention that Communism has to be seen in perspective. There are vital, substantive differences between the anti-Communist perception of Communism and the reality itself. It is necessary to separate the myth from the reality. To that task we shall eventually turn, but first let us look at the results of the anti-Communist mentality.

3. WHAT IT DOES TO US: Consequences of Anti-Communism in Domestic and Foreign Policy

AS A BASIC THEME in postwar American politics, anti-Communism has been both self-defeating and amoral. Rigid opposition to change and uncritical support for the status quo have been viewed as legitimate. Alternatives were defined in moralistic either/or terms of good versus evil, and it followed that basically democratic, humanitarian, tolerant measures and ideals that did not fit these narrow categories were condemned through a process of guilt by association.

The resort to guilt by labeling as a reactionary tactic against reform did not originate in the Cold War period, but the nature of postwar American domestic and international politics has been influenced drastically by the adoption of an anti-Communist—that is, anti-Soviet, anti-Chinese, antirevolutionary—rhetoric and approach. The rhetoric of American politics and the nature of American policy responses made anti-Communism a credo. Since it is an American development with historical causes, anti-Communism is neither inevitable nor irreversible. And even though the American public has adopted an anti-Communist credo, it should be sensitive to the ways this credo has influenced democratic ideals. An analytic review of the process and consequences of anti-Communism can create the basis for a re-evaluation of the anti-Communist approach. It is the purpose of this chapter to provide that analytic review.

I

The American Communist Party, despite intensive political activity and opportunity offered by the Great Depression, never became a serious political force in the United States. The American economic and social system, with all its weaknesses, has been sufficiently stable and resilient so that Communism has never been able to establish roots here as in underdeveloped countries where revolutionary situations prevailed.

In 1967 the U.S. Department of Justice (in which J. Edgar

Hoover directs the FBI) bowed to adverse Supreme Court and other judicial rulings and gave up its efforts to enforce the 1950 Internal Security Act's unconstitutional provision that the Communist Party and its members register as Soviet agents. "The Communist Party," said *The New York Times* editorially, "was never a major force in American life even at its peak in the 1930's and 1940's. Today it is an evanescent shadow, its small membership composed mainly of FBI agents, old people trapped by ancient loyalties, and a handful of young people, some of them children or grandchildren of veteran Party members. In the trade unions and in the intellectual community, where the Party once did have spotty influence, its role today is negligible. Even the revival of protest movements in the wake of recent civil rights and anti-Vietnam War struggles has done little to revivify it." [1]

Incontrovertible is the conclusion that our own society is not the soil in which Communism grows. Most Americans have a considerable stake in our social order with no interest in radically changing it. Even those Americans who have the smallest stake, or none at all, are so persistently hopeful in the land of opportunity that Communism has no attraction for them. If any segment of our population were to be susceptible to its blandishments, it would be the cruelly disadvantaged Negroes; but our handful of domestic Communist propagandists and recruiters have never been able to make a significant impact on them. Even the urban riots of 1966 and 1967 show no evidence of Communist leadership.

There have been, and still are, Communists in the United States bent upon the overthrow or subversion of our form of government. In the nature of the case, they try to penetrate our institutions and organizations, public and private, and to capture them, but with uniform unsuccess. There is not now and never has been, not even at the depths of the Great Depression, an appreciable acceptance of their ideology in any stratum of American society, or a significant sympathy for their programs or procedures. Even so respectable a doctrine as Socialism, represented by the eminent Norman Thomas, has failed phenomenally to find any support (in or out of public office). No doubt the reason for this, in part, is that many of Socialism's proposals, as Thomas himself has observed, were adopted by the New Deal.

Half a century's experience reveals that "the Red menace," the fear that American Communism represented a major threat to American capitalism, is a myth and should be laid to rest. Com-

[1] *The New York Times,* April 8, 1967.

munism's charges and rhetoric lacked appeal to a basically democratic public committed to gradual reform and private property. As such, the American Communist Party never posed any real strategic danger to the American political system (nor did the Communists effectively infiltrate the federal bureaucracy) even during the period when its commitments and loyalties were strongly bent toward the Soviet Union. Still the public came to perceive Communism as a real threat in the realm of sabotage or espionage; it feared that through Communist infiltration of the federal government the Communists might use their influence and position to subvert the interest of the United States.

This fear was hypothetical and without reality. Although dramatic, unproven charges were publicized by Congressional hearings in the 1940's and 1950's, an effective Communist spy ring never was able to operate in the United States. Nonetheless, the European experience during the 1930's and the essentially psychological commitment of American Communist Party members to the Soviet Union made Communist Party membership by federal employees seem a legitimate internal security concern for the federal government. Accordingly, efforts were made to exclude from federal employment individuals who were former or present members of the Communist Party or Communist-front action organizations. This process of political "purification" began during World War II, the bases for its inception being an executive directive of President Roosevelt and the Hatch and Smith Acts. A formal, permanent program was established only in March 1947 by President Harry S. Truman—the Federal Employees Loyalty Program.

When it began, Truman's loyalty program had a narrowly defined, specific purpose—to prevent espionage, sabotage or, stated more generally, spying. Yet the more outspoken advocates of a loyalty program saw in this a way to ferret out from federal employment liberals who espoused reformist ideals. By labeling individual beliefs and associations as subversive, the means could be provided not only to undercut reform but also to repeal or discredit the New Deal. Indeed, the focus of the hearings of 1947–48 of the House Committee on Un-American Activities was on Communist infiltration of the New Deal. Although the hearings were formally called a review of Communist espionage in the United States, the intent of the committee was to document Communist infiltration of the New Deal and the role that Communists played in the formulation, development, and execution of the New Deal policies. The real target was New Deal reformism rather than Communism.

By establishing a loyalty program, Truman, in part, sought to thwart the Red-baiting of reformers. He believed an executive-directed program that eliminated security risks from the Administration could thwart the investigation efforts of the more conservative Eightieth Congress by removing the subversion-espionage issue. The House Committee on Un-American Activities, as its hearings in 1947 and pre-November 1948 illustrated, was far more concerned about the reforms instituted during the New Deal than the question of sabotage or espionage. Truman's loyalty program sought to dramatize the fact that New Dealers were not Communists. The concerns of the President were both partisan and principled; to remove a campaign issue and to insure absolute security.

Truman's loyalty program did encourage more extensive and intensive political investigations. It did so, perhaps inadvertently, by reason of the vague and repressive procedures established for judging individual loyalty, and Truman's failure to define explicitly the limited nature and objectives of the program. Overt, disloyal acts, not past political activities or beliefs, were supposed to be the basis for dismissal.

As an investigative tactic, however, the employee's past associations and activities were subject to surveillance. If questionable activities were uncovered, a more intensive investigation was then to be initiated. Finally, a system of review boards was established enabling the employee to present his case and to appeal decisions, but the employee was denied access to the records on which dismissal charges were based. Following initial investigations, certain organizations were proscribed by the Attorney General as Communist-action or front organizations.

In the procedures that developed, there was a steady deterioration of what was taken to constitute guilt. First, the performer of deliberate actions was held culpable. Then, the sharp line between an act and an intention was erased, and men were judged guilty not because they *did* something but because they *might* do something. A man's intentions were presumed known, on the basis of the persons he mingled with or the organizations he joined.

The Attorney General, without holding open proceedings that permitted countertestimony and evidence, retained the sole right to review, judge, and list an organization. And although an organization could appeal to secure declassification, the procedure proscribed an organization as guilty unless it could conclusively establish its innocence. Prosecution acquired priority over individual rights. The Justice Department, whose expertise had been limited to the investigation of criminal activities, suddenly became the arbiter in the field of internal security. Individual membership in suspect organizations, while not stated as sufficient to confirm disloyalty, came to imply or suggest disloyalty. Inevitably, this administrative labeling procedure served to give the imprimatur to particular organizations as safe, along with their ideas and ideals. Other organizations were stigmatized as suspect.

A second basis for judging individual loyalty, in furtherance of the program's limited objective of determining dismissal or clearance, was the formal FBI loyalty report compiled after an intensive field examination. The FBI investigative report, though it acquired an aura of solid, impartial research and investigation, was actually a loose collection of unevaluated judgments about the individual, consisting of both investigative summaries of FBI agents and unsubstantiated comments and charges made by private citizens. No distinction was made between fact and allegation; all became part of the record, and the fact that much of the information comprising the loyalty report was groundless or false was not duly noted.

The House Committee on Un-American Activities, along with a number of legislative committees—including the Senate Internal Security Subcommittee and the Government Operations Committee —used their power to dole out punishment. Hiding behind Congressional immunity and refusing to give an accused witness the right to cross-examine, these committees stigmatized thousands of alleged subversives and cost innumerable people their jobs or their standing in the community.

Information given these committees has been proved unreliable on hundreds of occasions; it was unchecked and unedited, often based on testimony by informers fearful of deportation or prosecution for various crimes unless they testified against erstwhile associates. Yet HUAC admitted in 1949 that it had dossiers on more than a million people, presumably subversives. That the files are used for punishment is attested to by the fact that from 1949 to 1959 the committee furnished data on sixty thousand individuals and twelve thousand organizations to inquiring employers. In addition HUAC published a "Cumulative Index" and supplement, listing some forty-five thousand individuals and thousands of organizations mentioned in its hearings. This has been a handy reference for blacklisters and has cast a pall over many would-be dissenters. It made men fearful to join such mildly liberal organizations as the American Civil Liberties Union or the National Association for the Advancement of Colored People.

Truman failed to make clear the unevaluated nature of the information in federal and FBI reports. In failing to do so, he added credence to what were often incredible reports when he subsequently (March 1948) issued an executive directive prohibiting the divulgence of information contained in the loyalty reports to Congressional committees or to the public. These questionable reports became controversial, since their contents leaked to individual members of Congress, notably Senator Joseph McCarthy, who had a field day with his fluctuating charges of the continued employment of Communists in government.

On February 9, 1950, McCarthy said in a speech in Wheeling, West Virginia: "I have in my hand a list of 205 that were known to the Secretary of State as being members of the Communist Party and who, nevertheless, are still working and shaping the policy of the State Department." [2]

The next night in Salt Lake City, he said: "Last night I discussed the Communists in the State Department. I stated that I had the names of fifty-seven card-carrying members of the Communist Party." [3] Thereafter the number rose and fell with the occasion.

Wheeling's 205 gave way to the 57 of Salt Lake City and Reno; to the 81 of February 20; to the 10 of the open Tydings Committee hearings; to the 116 of the executive sessions; to 1 when he said he would stand or fall on the single case of Owen Lattimore; to 121 in the closing phases of the investigation; to the 106 of a Senate speech on June 6.[4] McCarthy employed what Richard Rovere has termed "the multiple untruth," which created for the Wisconsin Senator "an audience he would not have had if he had been a simpler and more modest liar." [5]

Responding to the McCarthy-induced pressure for a more effective loyalty program, Truman in 1951 amended the standard for dismissal of federal employees under his loyalty program. As originally established the program reflected a concern to insure against the abuse of loyalty charges and provided that dismissal should be based on hard evidence that "reasonable *grounds* exist for the belief that the person involved is *disloyal* to the government of the United States." The revised loyalty standard (April 1951) stipulated that "reasonable *doubt* exists as to the loyalty of the individual involved

[2] Frank Desmond's report in the Wheeling *Intelligencer,* quoted in Richard Rovere, *Senator Joe McCarthy,* p. 125.
[3] *Ibid.,* p. 128.
[4] *Ibid.,* p. 130.
[5] *Ibid.,* p. 139.

to the government of the United States." The changes from grounds to doubt and from disloyalty to loyalty were not semantic; rather they reflected a different set of priorities and expedited dismissal of suspect individuals. The very establishment of the program served to alter priorities, instituting a process of deterioration of what constituted loyalty.

First, these loyalty investigations consecrated the particular views as to what constitutes loyalty held by individual members of the Loyalty Review Board. They accredited anti-Communism per se, and they discredited certain radical ideas and political associations. The aura created promoted an attitude of playing it safe. Individuals became aware of what their associates and organizational affiliations might mean for their future. Reformist programs and movements became suspect since their objectives were taken to be undercutting the status quo. Dissent and radical criticism were silenced summarily, not through absence of merit but by the presence of fear. The tolerant atmosphere that fosters innovation and change was stifled, and complacency was created at a time when critical socio-economic problems required urgent attention.

The FBI's investigative role in the conduct of the loyalty program and its concern to insure against "Communist subversion" brought new popular respect for this agency; its investigations and pronouncements came to be mistakenly regarded as impartial and objective. As its activities, influence, and appropriations increased, its investigative judgments spilled over into the political realm. Politicians found it important and expedient to proclaim their hatred of Communism. Even more important, however, was the sanctification of the FBI and its director, along with the removal of the agency from traditional surveillance security.

Second, the nature of this anti-Communist obsession emphasized *absolute security*. When Truman first established the loyalty program, he suggested that the existence of even one disloyal employee constituted a grave threat to the national security. This rhetoric remains, justifying the resort even to wiretapping surveillance in areas of national security. It also has served to create impossible standards and a new set of priorities. Absolute security is impossible, but the attempt to achieve it has instituted a set of procedures corrosive of individual liberties. On the one hand, public fears have been intensified by the new definition of loyalty, and on the other hand, distinctly repressive standards for judging loyalty came to be accepted.

For the first time in peacetime history, loyalty and security programs had become part of the American scene. The Atomic Energy Act of 1946 required a rigorous screening of employees for character, associations, and loyalty. In the first five years of President Truman's loyalty program for *all* federal employees, the FBI, according to Director Hoover, processed four million applications for government jobs. A check for loyalty was instituted on those moving into federal housing projects and those working on jobs in private industry where defense production was taking place. A million tenants in government-sponsored homes had to sign loyalty oaths. Some were evicted for failing to comply. The Magnuson Act provided that merchant seamen and many longshoremen be cleared for security.

A far more immediate result of the investigations, directly affecting the domestic political climate, was the extension of the Loyalty Program to the broader American political scene. The Federal Employees Loyalty Program encouraged and justified a loyalty oath crusade on local and state levels that extended to the private sector, including the legal profession and private industry. Hundreds of thousands of teachers, professors and other employees were required to sign oaths that they were not Communists or subversives. In Indiana boxers and wrestlers had to attest to their loyalty before being permitted to fight or wrestle. Loyalty protestations became institutionalized rituals by which the individual citizen established his loyalty and disclaimed certain kinds of vaguely defined affiliations in order to affirm his patriotism. This virus still afflicts the body politic, as current attacks on proponents of civil rights and anti-Vietnam demonstrators illustrate. A dramatic case is the Pentagon's response to recent changes in the Confession of the Presbyterian Church.

After much debate and deliberation, the General Assembly of the United Presbyterian Church in the U.S.A. adopted a new creed, its first major doctrinal change since 1706, the "Confession of 1967," establishing social action as a basic part of church doctrine. This new confessional emphasizes the role of the church in the modern world. In political terms, the new creed provides church support and respectability for movements in the fields of civil rights and peace and other activities seeking to change the focus and direction of American society.

The section dealing with "Reconciliation in Society" proved troublesome. It read in part: "The church, in its own life, is called to practice the forgiveness of enemies and to commend to the nations as practical politics the search for cooperation and peace.

This requires the pursuit of fresh and responsible relations across every line of conflict, even at risk to national security, to reduce areas of strife and to broaden international understanding. Reconciliation among nations becomes peculiarly urgent as countries develop nuclear, chemical, and biological weapons, diverting their resources from constructive uses and risking the annihilation of mankind. Although nations may serve God's purpose in history, the church which identifies the sovereignty of any one nation or any one way of life with the cause of God denies the Lordship of Christ and betrays its calling."

The phrase "even at risk to national security" made the "Confession of 1967" a concern of loyalty for Pentagon personnel. In a May 23, 1967, article in *The New York Times,* Lawrence E. Davies reported that while the Confession was still under discussion by the General Assembly of the Church, a Pentagon official found it necessary to circulate a memorandum among military agencies and defense industries *denying* that adoption of the Confession would jeopardize the security clearance of members.[6]

The Presbyterian episode dramatically symbolizes the domestic consequences of the anti-Communist loyalty program. At issue, obviously, is not the overt disloyal acts of an individual but a process labeling certain beliefs as reflecting possible subversive proclivities. Such an approach has characterized the domestic anti-Communist program. It has culminated in a political situation wherein demands for change and reform can be discredited not because they lack merit or relevance but simply because they would reorder the status quo. Anti-Communism further has encouraged the reaction of the radical right, the most militantly antireformist sector of American society. The common emphasis of the diverse and quite numerous right-wing organizations—whether the John Birch Society, the White Citizens Council, the Minutemen—is formal and assertive anti-Communism. While rigidly anti-Soviet, their main conception of the Communist threat is internal, not external.

Indicative of this type of response was the effort of a right-wing group (the Concerned Catholic Parents) in the Chicago area to discredit a recently proposed archdiocesan third-grade catechism.

[6] An effort made in May 1968 by a Texas presbytery to delete the "treasonous" phrase prompted the ecumenical weekly, *The Christian Century,* to editorialize: "No doubt the Pentagon realized that it had no reason for alarm; alas, if and when the chips are down, not just Texas Presbyterians, not just most Presbyterians, but most Christians of whatever affiliation would no doubt prove to be idolaters at the shrine of the nation-state." *The Christian Century,* May 15, 1968, p. 641.

This catechism made positive reference to the civil rights movement, particularly to the leadership of the Reverend Martin Luther King, Jr.; therefore this group protested and futilely demanded that the FBI and the Chicago Police Department's Subversive Unit investigate the Roman Catholic Archdiocese of Chicago. Thus, under the cover of anti-Communism and national security, moral ideas and liberal social principles are castigated or declared anathema.

Of a far more serious nature has been the amending of the McCarran Internal Security Act of 1950. President Truman had vetoed the bill on the grounds "It would put the U.S. into the thought control business. It could give government officials vast powers to harass all of our citizens in the exercise of their rights of free speech." Congress was in no mood to listen, however, and it overrode the President's veto. The McCarran Act required "Communist," "Communist-front," and "Communist-infiltrated" organizations to register with the Attorney General, turn over membership lists, and label their written material "Communist." Individual members of such suspect organizations were prohibited from applying for passports or holding posts with a trade union or a defense industry. If they were noncitizens, they could be deported; and if recently naturalized, they could be denaturalized. The penalties for nonregistration were stringent—$10,000 in fines and five years in prison for *each day* that a "subversive" leader failed to register his movement.

Under the McCarran Act the Attorney General was empowered, in times of emergency, to detain any person against whom "there is reasonable ground to believe that such persons *probably* will engage in or *probably* will conspire with others to engage in acts of espionage or sabotage" (italics added). Although this remarkable section has never been used, it gives the government and the FBI the right to hold anyone it suspects without trial or any other judicial safeguard. J. Edgar Hoover was reported as saying in 1950 that he was prepared to arrest twelve thousand alleged enemy agents as soon as war broke out.

Although the act originally required Communists and front organizations to register with the government, none registered; and the Supreme Court ruled that self-registration was unconstitutional since it amounted to self-incrimination. This left the Subversive Activities Control Board with nothing to do. A bill passed by both houses of Congress (by a vote of 3 to 2 in the Senate with ninety-five Senators absent) empowers the SACB to hold hearings to decide what organizations are Communist fronts and then to publish the names of their members in a formal roster of Communists. The bill was signed into law by President Johnson on January 2, 1968.

The House bill was produced by the House Un-American Activities Committee, and the Senate bill was sponsored by Senator Everett Dirksen. In speaking of his bill, Senator Dirksen said: "The time for fooling is past. We have 475,000 youngsters and oldsters in Vietnam. What do you think they think when they read about these things going on in the Senate—people trying to stop the Subversive Activities Control Board from doing its work? What does the Senate think the North Vietnamese and Vietcong are composed of, if they are not Reds? . . . Are we going to . . . let them [domestic Communists] run loose here in this country, or are we going to come to grips with them?" [7]

The commitment to absolute "security" has restricted domestic and international development programs. Even so rich a country as the United States must limit over-all spending, for to the extent that military spending and internal security assume priority, other programs are demoted to secondary financial support.

A corollary of this process has been the concern for national security that has prompted the press and the mass media to cover up the excesses or mistakes of the government. Most noteworthy has been the role of the press in covering the activities of the Justice Department and the Central Intelligence Agency. For illustration, it suffices to list one case: a *New York Times* editorial decision. Though aware of the CIA's role in preparation for the Bay of Pigs invasion, *The Times* withheld the story on grounds of national security. The decision reflected a commitment not to inform the public of Administration misdoings and falsehoods even when unpublicized executive actions might involve the United States in a major undeclared war. Rather, *The Times* withheld the story so that the invasion might occur, fearing that disclosure might insure defeat and put the onus on *The Times* for undermining national security. Rather than serve as an independent agency disseminating public information and critically analyzing Administration decisions, *The Times* surrendered to the Administration's self-interpretation of what constituted the national interest.[8]

The Bay of Pigs incident is neither isolated nor unrepresentative.

[7] *The New York Times,* October 12, 1967.
[8] For a detailed examination of this delinquence of the press, see Victor Bernstein and Jesse Gordon, "The Press and the Bay of Pigs," *The Columbia University Forum,* Fall 1967.

The news media often have tacitly abandoned their responsibility as independent nongovernmental agencies providing the information necessary for the public to form critical judgments on the validity and desirability of Administration policy. Instead, the media have often become apologists for current policy. In the Cold War, the Administration has not resorted to censorship of the news on national security grounds. This has not been necessary: The press has been too often a willing and unsolicited supporter of government policy, deleting "undesirable" news and transmitting misinformation.

As one example, *Time* magazine on September 20, 1963, ran a story that was highly critical of the job done by press correspondents in South Vietnam. The report charged foreign correspondents in Saigon with pooling their misinformation and grievances, with being lacking in independent thought, with adding to South Vietnam's confusion, with filing distorted news stories. In other words, the newsmen in Saigon did not know what they were talking about, and the government reports were more reliable. So *Time* magazine stated, "Many of the correspondents seem reluctant to give splash treatment to anything that smacks of military victory in the ugly war against the Communists, since this weakens the argument that defeat is inevitable as long as Diem is in power."

Two *Time* correspondents quit in protest of that article. Charles Mohr, the magazine's Southeast Asia Bureau Chief, and Merton Perry, *Time*'s senior American correspondent in Vietnam, said, "The article was written entirely in New York without any report from Saigon . . . its description of the way newsmen here work was in sharp contrast to a long report that they submitted weeks earlier which was not used." [8a]

Press releases from the State and Defense Departments are regularly printed as fact with no effort made to check the accuracy of the releases. Richard L. Tobin, communications editor of *Saturday Review,* commenting on this trend a few years ago wrote: "There's been a general tendency since January 20, 1961, to 'manage' the news, to suppress facts, to control public information and to give the Pentagon in particular a sort of godlike role of judge and jury over what the American people ought to know." [9]

In justifying the government's manipulation of news, Arthur Sylvester, former Assistant Secretary of Defense, said, "I can't think of a comparable situation but in the kind of world we live in, the

[8a] *The New York Times,* October 4, 1963.
[9] *Saturday Review,* December 8, 1962, p. 62.

generation of news by government becomes one weapon in a strained situation." [10]

During the Cuban missile crisis in 1962, the Defense Department released a false story to confuse the Russians. Later, Arthur Sylvester reasons, "It would seem basic all through history, that a government's right . . . to lie and save itself when it is facing up to a nuclear war." [11] More recently, apropos of the Pueblo incident, when the veracity of the official United States version of the affair was questioned, Sylvester conceded that the occasions when the government has a right to lie "are rare, and if mishandled will damage rather than protect the country." [12] Still it is beyond debate that a nation which practices dishonesty on occasion will find the occasions increasing when it becomes handy to bend the truth. As J. R. Wiggins, editor of the Washington *Post,* has written, "A government that too readily rationalizes its right to lie in a crisis will never lack for either lies or crises." [13]

The management of the news has crippled the functioning of democracy in the foreign policy realm. Denied access to the record, the public has seen events through distorted lenses. Ignorant of alternatives, it has uncritically accepted policy pronouncements; it has perceived revolutions and Soviet/Chinese policy in the emotional way they have been reported. The tone and commitment of the press has inadvertently, but effectively, undermined the tolerance essential for a realistic debate on foreign policy. Only recently has a beginning been made in a more searching analysis of foreign policy.

Another consequence of the anti-Communist approach has been the weakening of Congressional and public restraints on the President's authority over foreign policy. Crisis diplomacy, requiring quick decision to halt the spread of Communism, has resulted in a strong, independently operating executive who ignores the constitutional restraints of debate before involving the nation in war.

The degree to which traditional constitutional concepts have been discarded by high administrative officers was indicated by the testimony of Nicholas Katzenbach, Undersecretary of State, in testimony before the Senate Foreign Relations Committee in August

[10] Washington *Star,* October 31, 1962, defending a policy of news management in an October 27 memorandum.

[11] Speech before New York Deadline Club, quoted in *Aviation Week,* December 17, 1962.

[12] *The New York Times,* February 6, 1968.

[13] Quoted in William McCaffin and Edwin Knoll, "The White House Lies," *The Progressive,* September 1967, p. 12.

1967. Addressing himself to United States involvement in Vietnam, Mr. Katzenbach dismissed the idea of a declaration of war voted by Congress with, "In this kind of context I think the expression of declaring war is one that has become outmoded in the international arena." [14]

Not only has much of the press been far from objective in its reporting of the Vietnam War, but many of those in Congress have refused to take their constitutional responsibility to heart and critically examine our foreign policy, particularly in Vietnam, and come up with constructive alternatives. Many Congressmen have allowed themselves to be used as rubber stamps to Administration policies as long as they are anti-Communist. Accepting arguments on the necessity of resolute action and the greater expertise of the Administration, the public and the Congress have forfeited their right and obligation to examine critically far-reaching executive policy decisions. The check-and-balance system of American politics has been altered in the realm of foreign policy, although, happily, some members of Congress, particularly in the Senate Foreign Relations Committee, are beginning to assert themselves. But an imbalance has ensued, justified and accepted on the nebulous grounds of anti-Communism and national security. The Administration has increasingly adopted an elitist approach in national security matters, both foreign and domestic, suggesting that secrecy is essential to the national security and that the public and the Congress, being ignorant, cannot form sound judgments on policy matters. So, in the name of national security, democracy has been undermined at home.

The extent to which decisions are made at executive levels while legislative channels are bypassed is revealed by the experience of the Chairman of the Senate Foreign Relations Committee. The Senate has the responsibility to review the conduct of foreign policy of the President and his advisers and then to offer advice as well as to grant or withhold its consent to major acts of foreign policy. Senator J. William Fulbright tells how he chanced to hear of the Bay of Pigs expedition in the spring of 1961. While aboard the Presidential plane on the way to Florida, he heard the President's advisers talking of the coming invasion. In Fulbright's words, "I was the only Senator involved in the fateful deliberation preceding the Bay of Pigs and my involvement was an accident." [15] Of American troops rushed to the Dominican Republic in April 1965, he wrote, ruing the fact that Congressional leaders were briefed

[14] *The New York Times,* August 18, 1967.
[15] J. William Fulbright, *The Arrogance of Power,* pp. 43–44.

about events and not consulted, "Had I known in April what I knew in August [after intensive review of the Dominican crisis by the Foreign Relations Committee], I most certainly would have objected to American intervention." [16]

Associated with the obsession that sees Communism anywhere as a threat to national security has been the changing role of power internationally. In the period after World War II, an emphasis on political diplomacy has become an emphasis on military power and a belief in United States omniscience and the benevolence of American interventionism. We are convinced that military action can contain Communism and that military acts, aid, or alliances are good-in-themselves. Thus, military intervention is accepted on strictly anti-Communist grounds, and United States troops in a variety of places are supporting hopelessly corrupt, repressive regimes unable to sustain their power without the United States military presence. The sole rationale for these actions has been the importance of containing or thwarting a Communist move.

The primacy of military aid, military sales (a billion and a half dollars a year), and an overwhelming power controlled by the United States, far from humbling the United States, has created a political climate justifying this power along with the belief that the failure to impose a military settlement or to defeat all "Communist" revolutions reflects a form of weakness, appeasement, and a betrayal of our responsibility as the leader of the Christian free world. In short, not only have principles become subservient to power, but the failure to use power ruthlessly is regarded as immoral, in opposition to an earlier view reflected in the concept of the just war.

This attitude has been followed by a dangerous trend of kowtowing before the expertise of the military. The generals have acquired new respect now that a Cold War against Communism has become hot and violent in Vietnam. Debate on disarmament and the 1962 test ban treaty involved the military as experts: Whether the military leaders' views were objective or reflected their service commitment was ignored. Although it is a firm American principle that the military must be properly subservient to the civilian sector, the position is now openly advanced that the military is the best, if not the only, judge of the national interest. This thesis was advanced by former Senator Barry Goldwater in the 1964 Presidential campaign; it was the basis for the bitter reaction to President Truman's dismissal of General MacArthur in April 1951.

[16] *Ibid.*, pp. 49–50.

More recently it has been persistently involved in the argument for allowing the military free rein in the conduct of the Vietnam War.

Policy decisions entailing far more than military consequences have been made in this military context; and considerations to curtail military spending or slow the armaments race have been conducted in the climate of national security through power. Obviously this approach limits the options for diplomacy and political change. The tendency to regard the military as experts in general rather than as partisan advocates of their own special interests colors the postwar disarmament and diplomatic debate. The motto of the Air Force's Strategic Air Command, "Peace is our profession," points to the Orwellian fashion within which peace and security have come to be interpreted. The "more bang for a buck" slogan of the Eisenhower-Dulles Administration equally reflects this narrow view of international politics and peace.

In the fall of 1967 on the occasion of presenting a young soldier returning from Vietnam with the Congressional Medal of Honor, President Johnson said: "We recognize and always have recognized that there can be no military 'solution' to the problems of Southeast Asia. But we have also had to face the hard reality that only military power can bar aggression and make a political solution possible."

The separation of the uses of military power from those of politics prompted *The New Yorker* magazine to editorialize: "We doubt if it will hasten the day of negotiations [in Vietnam] to grant military power a freewheeling existence of its own; in fact, it is likely to induce a degree of deafness in picking up peace signals. Nor is an over-reliance on the use of force likely to insure negotiations (when, or if they come) that will be different in kind from those of pre-nuclear times. It is not inspiriting to contemplate the course of negotiations that come about through military pressures; they are over before they are begun, it being foreordained that the victor will lead from strength, while the vanquished, momentarily compliant, plots to live and fight another day." [17] The insistence on giving priority to the military aspects for peace can only lead to failure.

Similarly, our society has become locked into an ever-expanding armaments defense program. The perception of security as military superiority over Communism has intensified the development of new weapons, the acquisition of new defense systems, and the building of new military bases. Essentially this marks an open-

[17] *The New Yorker*, "The Talk of the Town," October 14, 1967.

ended commitment to increase military spending, while opposing
the elimination of bases and earlier outmoded programs.

Though the missile has made the bomber and overseas bases
relatively obsolete or of secondary importance, continued possession of the bomber and overseas bases seems important to what is
called defense primarily because they exist. To phase them out
would seem to reduce United States military capabilities and undercut our military effort and hence our security. The process has
resulted in a one-way street with no exit to other roads providing
better routes to peace. When security is conceived in military terms
alone, then defense cutbacks become unthinkable, and negotiations
and diplomacy are no longer live options. Although former Secretary of Defense Robert McNamara had a cost-efficiency approach
to military spending, advocating cutbacks and slowdowns in certain areas, it is precisely here that the greatest pressure was
brought against him by superpatriotic and anti-Communist arguments.

The confluence of various forces presses a willing public toward
a military solution for the world problems. What President Eisenhower termed "the military-industrial complex" keeps alive the
Communist peril, for an enormous military budget has happy economic consequences for nearly everybody. In the early days of the
Cold War the tempting economic possibilities of East-West tension
became apparent. Thus a newsmagazine commented: "Government planners figure they have found the magic formula for almost
endless good times. They now are beginning to wonder if there
may not be something to perpetual motion after all. . . . Cold
War is the catalyst. Cold War is an automatic pump primer. Turn
a spigot and the public clamors for more arms spending, turn another, the clamor ceases. . . . Cold War demands, if fully exploited, are almost limitless." [18] Today the armed forces have
three thousand men, world-wide, in its public affairs sections,
spreading propaganda that suits military interest, educating millions
of soldiers in its hawkish version of the present conflict, feeding
reams of material to the press and magazines.

But the use of international tension to promote prosperity is a
hazardous occupation. Former Secretary of Defense Charles W.
Wilson (not to be confused with the Wilson of General Electric)
said in 1957: "One of the most serious things about this defense
business is that so many Americans are getting a vested interest

[18] *U.S. News & World Report*, May 26, 1950, quoted in Victor H. Wallace
(ed.), *The Paths to Peace*, p. 73.

in it: properties, business, jobs, employment, votes, opportunities for promotion and advancement, bigger salaries for scientists, and all that. It is a troublesome business." [18a] President Eisenhower warned in his farewell address on January 17, 1961 that "this conjunction of an immense military establishment and a large armaments industry is new in the American experience. . . . The potential for the disastrous rise of misplaced power exists and will persist." Senator William Proxmire (D.-Wisc.) charged in April 1962 that the Pentagon had one lobbyist for each Senator and Congressman.

The military establishment has grown to proportions never before known in American life. Today it owns—conservatively—200 billion dollars in property, three times the combined wealth of U.S. Steel, General Motors, Metropolitan Life, American Telephone and Telegraph, and Standard Oil of New Jersey. In 1931 the military held three million acres of land; by 1959 the figure was thirty-one million, larger in area than the seven smallest states together. It spends upward of $25 billion a year on procurement and grants $6 to $8 billion to business for research and development and a billion to universities and colleges. As of 1960 it operated 3,553 military installations in the United States and more outside our borders.

There is a wholesale intertwining of the military with both government and big business. One estimate a few years ago held that thirteen hundred high military figures, retired or on leave, were working at key jobs in federal departments. In the 1966 Congress, a Congressional Reserve unit, headed by Air Force Major General Barry Goldwater and Army Brigadier General J. Strom Thurmond, numbered 175 members, about a third of Congress. According to a House subcommittee in 1961 there were fourteen hundred retired officers of the rank of major or higher (261 of them generals or admirals) employed in top capacities by the one hundred biggest defense corporations that share handsomely in the annual military budget, which now is $75 billion.

It is no accident, therefore, that there has been such a growth of rightist groups in the United States, or that they are financed by corporate interests, many of whom benefit from Cold War tensions. Or that, allied with the rightists, big business, and the military is another social stratum—what Professor Irving L. Horowitz called the "new civilian militarists." These writers and men of sci-

[18a] Quoted by Fred J. Cook, *The Warfare State,* p. 299.

ence, such as Edward Teller and Herman Kahn, lend an intellectual aura to military contentions.

From an earlier aversion to conscription and a large peacetime army, the postwar United States has come to accept uncritically the need for a peacetime selective service system. Increasingly, the debate on conscription has become a hollow one. The need for a standing army has been made plausible not by its successes in safeguarding or furthering the national security but simply because it exists, bolstered by the anti-Communist rhetoric.

Related to this form of militarism has been the transformation of the body politic's perception of violence and nonviolence. A military-oriented society, eulogizing force and committed to the status quo, supported by a political rhetoric of anti-Communism, diminishes the prospect for domestic change.

II

A direful consequence of this approach is an international arms race seen, in the most obvious sense, as the balance-counter-balance efforts of the United States and the Soviet Union in the nuclear field since 1945. In a less obvious sense, this approach has resulted in the United States becoming the arsenal for the world. To contain Communism, we have sold, lent, or supplied billions of dollars of arms to innumerable nations throughout the world. The Administration has sought to tie the defense systems of these nations into that of the United States. The result has been military conflict between these states that we have armed (India–Pakistan, Greece–Turkey, Israel–Jordan, the war over Kashmir, the war over Cyprus, and the war over the West Bank of the Jordan) and subversion of economic reform by diversion of resources needed for economic development to military spending (Peru, Argentina, Bolivia, Brazil). And, through the Country-X loans of the Export-Import Bank, the Defense Department has promoted the sale of American-made munitions to those underdeveloped countries lacking the capital to develop their own large, well-equipped standing armies and air forces.

The commitment to the machinery of war has created a far-flung *intelligence-gathering* organization, the Central Intelligence Agency. Originally limited to securing information on foreign subversive and military activities, this agency has spiralled in influence and function. No longer simply an intelligence agency, the CIA has exercised a policy-making function. Removed from public control, surveillance, and knowledge, its actions have proliferated; it is reputed to have between fifteen thousand and forty thousand employees and to spend between $400 million and $700 million a year. It has subsidized or directed revolutions, provoked labor strikes abroad, and compromised the independence of American professional and private organizations. Committed to the continuance of the Cold War, this agency has colored the intelligence it has passed on, thus restricting the Administration's options and alternative approaches to international problems. The CIA justified its subsidization of the National Student Association and other private organizations on the grounds that Congress never would have funded these programs knowingly. This explanation sounds harmless enough, but the CIA used the NSA as a means of recruiting agents, and it warned students not to take anti-Vietnam positions publicly. Through its secrecy and stealth the CIA has partially subverted the democratic process.

Our anti-Communist obsession distorts our priorities and commitments. The idea of negotiations from strength implies the primacy of power and the importance of atomic weapons as the means for insuring compliance with our objectives.

The existence of a standing army, made possible through the draft, has reduced the President's dependency on Congressional and public support for United States military action overseas. Using his powers as Commander-in-Chief, and relying on the rhetoric of containing Communism, the President can commit United States troops in disregard of Congressional foreign policy restraints. As a result, the Congress and the public reaffirm Presidential decisions not out of conviction; they simply don't want to embarrass him, or they blindly accept his anti-Communist rationale. Contrast the bitter debate that followed President Truman's use of his powers as Commander-in-Chief to direct United States military action in the Korean War with the more placid Congressional acceptance of Presidential action in Vietnam and the Dominican Republic.

The continuing Cold War has made certain actions acceptable to many people and has undermined former restraints on executive authority. The debate over the army and its role has subsided; the question of the size of the military budget has become meaningless. Budgetary priorities and the desire to avert inflation have had disastrous effects on domestic reform programs. The interest of the military-industrial complex in disarmament is inhibited by its economic and political interest in war and armaments.

The build-up of weapons proceeds without regard to need. If military strength is essential for defense, then the proliferation of hardware is no longer justified as promoting that limited end. A contemporary (1967) example reveals the warped perception of a blindly negative anti-Communist approach. France's disassociation from NATO and the lessening of Soviet control over Eastern Europe opened a new opportunity for American diplomacy in Europe. This opportunity was not pursued; opportunities for a meaningful détente and reduction in military spending have been bypassed by Congress. Instead, the same old assumptions, now programmed to these changes, have continued to govern policy decisions.

Taking advantage of easing military tensions in Europe, the Soviet Union has sought to woo the Western European nations away from dependence on the United States. The original need for NATO was attributed to Western European weakness and Soviet expansionism, and the objective was to insure an independent Europe; yet recent developments making possible an independent Europe were welcomed by neither the military nor the Administration. The reaction of certain NATO military officers to these trends reflects peculiar reasoning used by an uncritical, self-legitimizing, anti-Communist military policy. They reveal a reflex-type reaction against change, an inability to see that outworn assumptions about the Soviet Union and the primacy of power for insuring peace are no longer valid. The response on the part of American military officials to the more independent role of France, to British flirting with the Soviet Union, to West German interests in a military cutback, and to the prospects of mutual troop reductions in Europe, all illustrate this self-defeating view. American military officials have expressed the fear that such actions might lead to the reduction of troop strength by both the Soviet bloc and the European states and the possible eventual dissolution of NATO. The United States military do not question whether NATO should continue; its existence is sufficient justification for its continuance. Seemingly eager to maintain the old military-minded, anti-Communistic NATO pattern, the United States has fought efforts to reform NATO in accordance with new political realities.

The debate over the worth of an antiballistic-missile system reflects similar prejudices. Although the arms race has only increased our insecurity, new armaments expenditures are justified as necessary for defensive purposes. Crucial questions are dismissed: the probability of attack, the possibility the system will become outmoded before it becomes operative, effectiveness versus cost, the incitement of a new round of the arms race. Under the peculiar anti-Communist view of international politics now dominant, rational and moral thought seems difficult. Power is vaunted and every increase in weaponry is assumed to increase security, whereas in fact such increases in a nuclear age only edge us closer to doomsday. Secretary McNamara, apparently reluctant to initiate an anti-ballistic-missile system, was pressured to approve a "thin" system—the first step in another armament spiral.

Containing Communism has come to be the standard by which the Administration and the public judge events and formulate policies. So, although unstated, official United States policy has, in fact, become the supporter of a conservative status quo. Moreover, since the Communist threat and the anti-Communist response came to be defined in terms strictly of power politics, the form of the response became narrowly conservative and militaristic.

Rhetorically, United States policy has professed a commitment to remove the causes of discontent and to provide the opportunity and prospect for economic development (reform and democratic change), yet policy decisions have increasingly subordinated economic and political reform to military security and stability. The clearest commitment has been to secure military allies. Neutrality became anathema, and in order to secure United States aid, a foreign nation need only give uncritical support to United States foreign policy aims. Congressional foreign aid appropriations and the variety of postwar military agreements that were entered into by postwar administrations give evidence of a willingness to recognize, support, and co-operate with outspokenly anti-Communist military dictatorships. So neutralist and radical revolutionary movements were opposed and undercut. Economic aid became mostly contingent upon acceptance of the American model of economic development, American technical advice, and the support of American capital interests.

As anti-Communism became a foundation for American policy, a peculiar understanding of revolution and radicalism emerged: Efforts to change the established order through far-reaching reforms came to be viewed as indicating Communist action or influence. The United States has difficulty accepting changes in foreign countries if such changes might jeopardize an anti-Communist stance. And to the extent that the United States embarked upon an avowedly anti-Communist, antirevolutionary course, the prospects for gradual change in other countries were foreclosed and democratic-nationalist ideals were being battered down. The world became the arena for a rigid and senseless ideological conflict among the Great Powers. In the United States, partly through a misconception of the relevance of power, revolutionary change came to be identified with foreign aggression and subversion. Independent radicalism was dismissed as impossible and undesirable. And, since the initiative for social change was mistaken as Communist expansionism, any United States countermove became a moral crusade.

Minor crises of revolutionary developments in the Third World, which in no way threatened the security of the United States, were seen as jeopardizing our national interest. The domino theory was resurrected—the belief that unresisted revolution would encourage Communist expansionism and bring on World War III. To fight in Greece, or Korea, or Vietnam would prevent an invasion of California, or Alaska, or Hawaii. Radical change was seen as Soviet-directed (later Chinese-directed) subversion and the United States felt duty bound to thwart it. Attempts by the Soviet Union and native Communists to dominate or direct some revolutions seemed to justify a countervailing policy in which all revolution or political radicalism became anathema to the United States. Anti-Communist, Cold-War-oriented makers of American foreign policy were unable to accept the inevitability of revolution directed against oppressive regimes. Rather than understand the demand of former colonies for immediate liberation, they came to oppose them, preferring to cooperate with existing power structures while urging the leadership to institute needed reforms. This policy approach became counterproductive, for it insured an active Soviet role and precluded alternative options of native radicals who might wish to remain neutral toward Great Power rivalries.

Ironically, this policy approach has been self-defeating even if judged by its own standards of containing Communism. Negative anti-Communism has on occasion created Communists. The most vivid example of this is the American intervention in Vietnam. There, the military containment of Communism through support of an entrenched reactionary bureaucracy has served only to prevent needed political and economic change. National reformers have been forced to accept either the status quo or the leadership of the Communist-led National Liberation Front. An anti-Communist policy has been ruining the country and forcing into the National Liberation Front many Vietnamese seeking a better, less oppressive life.

Confirmation of this is found in the Defense Department's own statistics. In 1963 when United States troops numbered 3,164, the Vietcong had approximately 53,000 men. By 1965 United States troops had been increased to 181,000, while Vietcong strength had increased nearly four-fold to 230,000.[19] This was prior to any sizeable infiltration from the North. The expanding American presence, the bombing of villages, and the defoliation of crops has persuaded many Vietnamese that their only salvation lies in repelling the Americans from their land.

Malcolm W. Browne, who served for five years as a correspondent in Southeast Asia, writes, "The Vietcong has infiltrated the Vietnamese forces like termites in a rotten log. Some American intelligence men estimate that as many as 30 per cent of Saigon's officers and men actually are sympathizers or agents of the Vietcong." [20]

The same American build-up served to undercut other options, the most notable being that of the more militant Buddhists. And the United States Administration, while mouthing support for democracy and social change, became committed to the support of the ruling forces in Vietnam—the military and their retinues of civil servants, businessmen, and landowners—and indeed built the class of American-dependent profiteers to a size and strength it has never known before.

Branding revolution and radicalism as Soviet-directed subversion provided a convenient model for judging international developments, but it ignored the complexity of international politics and the underlying oppressive conditions in underdeveloped countries that lead to revolutions. American policy responses amounted to an unthinking reflex action: When in doubt, support the existing regime through military aid or, as in the case of Vietnam and the Dominican Republic, create a pro-American, anti-Communist, regime through direct United States military intervention. The effect of this policy necessarily has been to make minor crises major, distorting their true significance.

The United States, seeing the Soviet Union lurking behind every socially and politically distressed situation, became ill equipped to negotiate diplomatic settlements. To negotiate would imply appeasement and admit cowardice. This rigidity achieved neither security nor stability; rather it encouraged inflexibility on the part of the

[19] Figures from Appendix of *The War in Vietnam,* prepared by the Staff of the Senate Republican Policy Committee.
[20] Malcolm W. Browne, "Why South Vietnam's Army Won't Fight," *True,* October 1967.

Soviets, China, and native revolutionaries. Negotiation of differences seemed impossible to the United States, convinced both of
its own altruism and the sinister objectives of its adversary, and to
the Soviet Union, which professed to be the champion of revolution
and Marxism-Leninism. Attempts to resolve pressing international
problems diplomatically were frustrated, and nuclear arms-rattling
culminated in the Cuban missile crisis. This threatened a major
holocaust and delayed development in the Third World by reduc-
ing the possibilities for peaceful, democratic change.

The word "negotiation" itself has been vulgarized in recent years.
Although it still carries positive emotive force and connotes con-
ference-table adjudication of differences, in practice it seems to be
used by American government spokesmen to describe the situation
in which the North Vietnamese, battered by our bombing, are
willing to capitulate—on behalf of the National Liberation Front
as well—to the American concept of a divided Vietnam.

Socioeconomic reform has been inhibited in the Third World at
a time of rising expectations, while the gap between the developed
and underdeveloped nations steadily increases. The positive lines
along which the United States must deal with these basic socio-
economic problems have been drastically blurred as a result of our
anti-Communist policy since 1945. Our policy has polarized the international politics of Third World nation states, between a right-
wing military and a radical, anti-American revolutionary force.
Violent, often irrational outbursts on tribal or parochial lines have
been fomented by groups grown tired of poverty and exploitation.
Native democratic socialists are the most forgotten victims of our
anti-Communist foreign policy. Although they offer options for
democratic, peaceful reform, the democratic socialists lack either
the military means or the ability to influence the politics of their
own nation states caught in a Cold War. Under these conditions,
power becomes supreme, and the situation is aggravated when the
regime in office is armed and supplied by a major power.

The United States, despite its enunciated ideals and aims, has
ignored the middle option or, through earlier commitments, has
frustrated that option. We face a bleak situation for long-term
United States interest. Hampered by its misreading of current
events, the United States can offer little to the social idealists of the
Third World. In fact, for many it has come to symbolize the very
forces and influences that nationalist revolutionaries seek to overthrow. In the Third World, consequently, anti-Americanism has
become as effective a political symbol as has anti-Communism in

the United States. This deep-seated distrust excludes a sensitive and constructive major United States role, causing some governments to hesitate to accept our aid. At the same time, this process of alienation serves to validate the arguments of American opponents of reform, those unrelenting supporters of the status quo. Thus American conservatives have demanded an end to the United States embargo on anti-Communist Rhodesia. To them, South Africa poses as the champion of order and anti-Communism.

CONCLUSION

The great gulf between conventional American political imagery and the realities all around explains in part the profound malaise of American youth today. The sharp protests of the New Left derive their strength from the failure of American society to live up to its humanitarian ideals. To the New Left, the promise of American life has become a fraud; the moralism of their parents and existing liberal leadership, that is, The Establishment, seem hypocritical and subversive of traditional American ideals. In a curious way, one can also see that the nihilism and extremism of young American conservatives reflect their protest against the failure of the United States to win victory over godless Communism. The hesitation of the government to use American power to the fullest, despite its rhetoric of confrontation with Communism, produces an alienation on the right, which is aggravated by the alleged socialization or Communization of the United States through government intervention via social legislation.

The alienation of American youth of both the left and the right, together with alienation and subversion of the revolutionary aspirations of exploited underdeveloped nations, dramatically points up the unfortunate legacies of anti-Communism. These consequences of a blind, emotional anti-Communism pose the most critical problem that American society presently confronts. Because it is based on fear and reflects frustration with change, the anti-Communist credo offers no solutions to basic domestic and foreign problems. A new approach is needed that is more positively committed to humanitarian and democratic change.

The fruits of anti-Communist frenzy have reduced the ability of our society to recognize real Communism and confront it effectively; in fifty years, starting with nothing but an idea and a handful of adherents, Communism has come into power over more than a third of the world. In America Communism has been able to do nothing more than win (and then mostly lose) a handful of converts. But anti-Communism has steadily reduced those domestic liberties, political, civil, and social, which no law, no court, no police force, and no army can save from an inflamed and worried people bent upon destroying them at home.

There is no evil that an external enemy can visit upon a nation which the nation cannot more easily visit upon itself—more easily and more durably. Free institutions, commanding the free devotion of a people, are not destroyed by conquest, but only by abdication. When the Danes were liberated in 1945, after five years of Nazi tyranny, they were able to restore their liberties intact and at once because they have never, even under the heel of the conqueror, lost their love of them.

I. F. Stone paints the picture of two hypothetical countries:

Country A did everything that could possibly be done to suppress Communism. It outlawed the party and the press. It required a loyalty oath of its people. Its secret police were everywhere. Its military were ruthless and were successfully used to break up meetings and demonstrations. Individual Communists were hunted down and imprisoned. No known Communist from abroad was allowed to enter Country A.

Country B, on the other hand, did nothing to stop Communism. The party and its press were legal and its meetings freely held. There were no loyalty oaths, no secret police, no arrests, no repression. Native Communists enjoyed every liberty and Communists from abroad were admitted to the country to carry on their activities without hindrance.

Which of these two countries was overthrown by Communism? Country A was Czarist Russia. Country B was England.

If, in the name of security, we destroy our liberties, what will we have secured? Why go to the trouble to oppose a foreign dictatorship, if, in the process, we install our own? The evils that anti-Communism has drawn in its train are inimical to liberty as Washington, Jefferson, and Lincoln understood liberty. The dread of the enemy without has aligned our government with regimes abroad that are as oppressive as the anti-Communists' Bolshevik. As Truman's policy sought to stop Communism in Greece, only to end in the submission of that country to dictatorship twenty years later, so too Johnson's policy of stopping the spread of Communism in Southeast Asia has, as its only certain success, the maintenance of a corrupt military tyranny over the people it thought to protect.

But perhaps the most pernicious consequence of doctrinaire anti-Communism—as it is of doctrinaire Communism—is its immeasurable effect on the humanity of each of us. If Communism (or capitalism) is evil incarnate and capitalism (or, conversely, Communism) unalloyed good, the protagonists of each ineluctably assume the form of incarnate and unalloyed evil in the eyes of the other—in the eyes, and in the hearts. Good and evil, right and wrong, saint and sinner, angel and devil cannot co-exist. They must fight to the end, and fight heartlessly.

Once we have persuaded ourselves that some men are saints and some sinners, forgetting that no man is a saint and that all men are sinners, the Armageddon attitude follows: Any and every means may, and indeed must, be used to win and to wipe out evil as ruthlessly as we would fight to wipe out plague. Our hearts *as men* become hardened, hardened to the point where we are compelled to ignore the obvious fact that the innocent bystanders in the struggle are its most defenseless and most numerous sufferers.

The technology of modern war conspires with this process to dehumanize the man on the other side, who becomes no longer a person like ourselves, with hopes and sorrows and responsibilities. The artillerymen who fire long-distance shells, rockets, and missiles, the aviators who drop their bombs from five miles above the clouds, never see the enemy. They never see what they have done to human beings. They never have to be haunted by the dying cries or whimpers of the mother or the child they have killed. The real nature of their act is hidden from them. They have played a game. Their instruments told them that they were on target, and they let go and scored a hit. The world has been rid of some more Communists.

But our soldiers' own mothers and fathers, wives and brothers and children at home are drawn into the deadly game as deeply as they. The enemy threatens the life of my loved one. Anything that hurts the enemy rejoices me. Let it be a bomb fragment, a bullet, or a bayonet; or let it be a famine, a flood, a drought, an earthquake, or a volcanic explosion or a fire. It has not hurt people; it has hurt the enemy. Communism is evil, and Russians are Communists; whatever injures Russians must be good in the struggle to the death between good and evil. The Vietcong body count is as satisfying as our own body count is distressing.

American insensitivity to the destruction of those human beings who wear a Communist label is illustrated by the American reaction to what happened in Indonesia in late 1965 and early 1966.

During about a six-month period Communists and suspected Communists were slain by the hundreds of thousands. The victims were machine-gunned, starved, decapitated; entire families were killed. Estimates of those massacred range from a conservative 300,000 to 500,000. The reaction of the American press? The blood bath was regarded as a smashing defeat for Communism. There was practically no deploring of the human tragedy involved.

We no longer think of people or of persons. We no longer think of the innocent bystander. We no longer think of mothers and children, or the old and the sick. We no longer think of the suffering of men like ourselves. We no longer think of Christ's answer to the question, "Who is my neighbor?" We no longer think. We accept the necessity for slaughter, and we become dehumanized ourselves. At home, in our cities and on our highways, in our schools and our living rooms, on our streets and our playgrounds, indifference to human life flourishes, as does indifference to the taking of human life. Imperceptibly we lose the capacity to consider life sacred and to assume our own divine responsibility to serve it and save it. "Love one another," Christ said, but we love only those who love us; we care nothing for those who do not love us, let them be avowed enemies or illiterate peasants who do not even know who we are.

The American terror of the enemy within has proved to be even more deadly than the terror of foreign attack. Public and private personages in all sincerity identifying libertarianism and social legislation with Communism have not only reduced political debate to an epithet but have, willy-nilly, engendered a pervasive mistrust among their fellow citizens. This mistrust in turn has evoked both customary and legal restrictions upon dissent and further reduced the level of public discussion.

As the threat of fire or flood has martial law as its immediate corollary, so the threat of subversion evokes submission to greater and greater government control in the area of civil liberties. Secret police forces at home and abroad take their place beside—and above—the uniformed police to whom we entrusted the protection of society before fear drove us mercilessly before it. Local and state controls give way to national controls as the only adequate means of combating the national threat; and the interaction of the domestic terror with the prospect of foreign attack by international Communism within less than a generation changes the face of a nation whose founding fathers warned it against the menace to liberty in great standing armies. We have become the garrison state that once horrified us in Europe and from which so many of our ancestors fled to the New World.

It was not a thousand years ago—as it may seem—but twenty that Senator Robert A. Taft, "Mr. Republican," insisted that there should be no discrimination in our educational system against a Communist as a school teacher. Compare that position, taken by one of the most eminent conservatives of modern history, with the finding, after fifteen years of Cold War, by the National Opinion Research Center in 1963 that 68 per cent of the American people would not allow a Communist to make a speech; 66 per cent would take his books out of the public libraries; 90 per cent would fire him from a defense plant job; 68 per cent would fire him from a clerk's job in a store; 91 per cent would fire him from a high school teaching post; 89 per cent would fire him from a college professorship; 77 per cent would take away his American citizenship; 61 per cent would put him in jail; and 64 per cent would give the government the right to listen to his private telephone conversations.

Perhaps "Mr. Republican" was a hidden Communist—and why not, if, as the founder of the John Birch Society said, President Eisenhower and Secretary of State Dulles were? Perhaps your neighbor, your friend, your father, your son, your husband. . . . This is the price that anti-Communism has exacted of us. The whole price has not yet been required. The whole price is the totalitarian tyranny, self-inflicted, against which we have meant to protect ourselves. Should we take our present course to its end, we shall discover its error only when it is too late.

And it is late. Quietly, without too much fanfare, fundamental democratic traditions have been eroded. As a basic trend in postwar American politics, anti-Communism has had a profound effect on American political values and policy responses. Democratic traditions that are being altered or have already been decisively modified are the following:

1. That a man must prove himself innocent, rather than that the state must prove him guilty beyond reasonable doubt.
2. That citizens may be effectively punished by executive or legislative committee decision rather than by judicial process.
3. That the state must be given greater protection against the citizen, rather than the other way around.
4. That the military, instead of being totally subordinate to civilian control, must be given greater autonomy.

5. That certain activities of the government are not subject to popular scrutiny or countervailing power.

6. That ideas presented by suspect individuals called "Communists," "Communist-sympathizers," "Fifth Amendment Communists," or "pinkos" are automatically wrong and need not be discussed.

7. That foreign policy is not a subject for national discussion, since the major parties adopt a bipartisan policy thus offering no choice to the electorate on the most important issue confronting them.

8. That citizens are guilty of crimes or near-crimes not because of what they do but because of what they say or think, or because of what is said or thought by men with whom they are associated.

9. That the state has a right secretly to infiltrate, finance, and control private institutions such as student or labor organizations.

10. That certain ideas and philosophies are automatically treasonous and their discussion is in itself criminal or treasonous.

11. That the checks-and-balances concept must be modified so that many key facts may be withheld from public knowledge, disguised, or even lied about by the government.

12. That the executive branch of the government can engage the nation in international commitments without going through the proper constitutional legislative channels.

This list of freedoms lost or jeopardized is a glaring illustration of the casualties brought about by an irrational anti-Communism intent on ferreting out and destroying an alien ideology but careless of the means employed. The consequent phobia has made America sick in body and soul.

4. WHAT IT REALLY IS: Anti-Communism—
Myth and Reality

THE PERCEPTIONS of anti-Communism are not totally false and un-
real; in such images there is enough correspondence with fact to
confirm the perceptions partially. The weakness of anti-Communism's perception lies in its incompleteness, oversimplification, and
distortion, emphasizing one set of elements while ignoring others.
It seeks out the re-enforcement of confirming events and rejects or
is blind to modifying or contradictory evidence.

Moreover, to say "Communism is . . ." is to oversimplify to
the point of falsehood, for Communism is a dynamic mixture of
ideology (both pro-something and anti-something). It is economic
attitudes and structures, political power states, and attitudes and
practices relating to revolution. When Communist countries or
movements are examined, their complexities and differences become even more apparent.

The factionalism of the Communist movement began with the
dispute between Lenin, on the one hand, and most of the rest of
the Party, including Stalin, on the other, over whether the "bourgeois revolution" of 1917 should be supported or whether the
Communists should accelerate toward a "proletarian revolution."
Succeeding disputes, each with high-pitched rhetoric, sometimes
caused permanent schism and involved such theoretical issues as
socialism in one country versus world revolution; the bloc of four
classes in China, co-operation versus independent action apart
from the Kuomintang; the strategy of relying essentially on the
urban working class versus the strategy of relying on the peasants;
bureaucratic Party management of industry versus technocratic
self-management, and innumerable others. There is just as much
difference between the various types of Communism that have
evolved—Leninism, Menshevism, Trotskyism, Bukharinism, Stalinism, Maoism, Titoism, Khrushchevism, and so on—as there is between capitalist theory for example in the United States and Portugal, or in the United States and Sweden.

IMAGES AND REALITIES

Anti-Communism's View of Communism

1. Communism is thought to be dedicated to the revolution of the poor, and to radical social and economic change. Although true of Communism in the past, and still true in theory, this view is much less valid today, because the Soviet Union, having achieved a large measure of economic well-being for its people, now has a vested interest in defending and protecting the status quo. Actually, the Soviet Union is moving rapidly into the family of the have nations and belongs to the privileged North rather than the dispossessed South.

There has emerged a mutuality of interests between the have nations and a simultaneous divergence between have and have-not nations independent of their political systems. Thus, negotiations are concluded enabling Western capitalist firms to build factories and assembly plants in the Soviet Union, and the Russians seek to win a public works contract in free-enterprise societies. This economic competitiveness is distinct from the relations between, for example, the Soviet Union and China or the United States and Brazil. Mutuality cannot be, because it has not been, based on common ideology or rhetoric. There is an unwillingness on the part of advantaged nations to promote self-sacrifice whether it be to secure self-determination or revolution for other peoples. This holds true for both the political idealism of the United States and the revolutionary rhetoric of the Soviet Union.

Not only has the Soviet Union failed to maintain dynamic leadership of radical revolution abroad, it has also failed to sustain continuing emphasis on radical revolution at home. Revolution means a radical restructuring of society toward equalization of power, status, and income. In that sense the U.S.S.R. and other European Communist countries as well do not have classless societies. Even the trends do not appear to be in that direction. The validity of the insistence by Milovan Djilas regarding the emergence of a "New Class" in Communist society is widely acknowledged. While income differences may not be as sharp as those of the West, they are pronounced and clear. Ebenstein and others have pointed out the emergence of a Communist salariat, which does not identify with the proletariat.[1]

[1] William Ebenstein, *Today's Isms: Communism, Fascism, Capitalism,* pp. 17–23, 53–54.

More recently China has insisted on revolution abroad and radical revolution at home. This fact leads to our second point.

2. Americans have commonly regarded Communism as monolithic, with directives from Moscow being carried out by disciplined Party members all over the world. To call Communism monolithic today probably has less justification than to call Western European countries monolithic. Undoubtedly, Communism as a system of ideas, as a political and an economic system, does have a central thrust, yet Communism at any given time reveals significant diversities. Recently, it has shown a growing trend toward decentralism, polycentrism, and variety—a trend which appears to be irreversible, and which even the invasion of Czechoslovakia will not stop.

Communism does not show the uniformity that most anti-Communists, and undoubtedly some Communists, would like to find. Words like "dialectic," "materialistic," "socialism," "imperialism," are used in such a variety of ways by speakers in different countries of different times that an objective observer cannot find a common meaning in them. The "ambiguous legacy," as Sidney Hook calls it, pervades the work of Marx and increases rather than diminishes with time. The phases of Marx—universal humanist as in the 1844 manuscripts; expectant revolutionist as in the period prior to 1848; and the later less optimistic, more cautious Marx of the English period—all these and more are revealed in later theoretical battles between center, right, and left. Even the key word "revolution" is sometimes used in the Copernican sense of "profound but peaceful change," and sometimes in the sense of rapid, violent seizure of political power.

The conflicts have never finished between activist-anarchists and organization men as in the First International, Bernsteinism revisionists and Orthodox Marxists like Katusky and Luxemburg, who later shifted position; between those who favor socialism in one country and socialism for export; between those who argue that they have arrived at a society without contradictions and those who see a long struggle ahead. There is disagreement as to whether *all* of humanity can be liberated from the shackles of irrational social organization, or only some portion of it; disagreement as to the means of this liberation; and disagreement as to whether the vehicle of this social transformation is the industrialized proletariat or the peasantry or, in fact, the Party itself. The attempt to trace the lineage of Marxism brings one into a bewildering maze of shifting coalitions, deviations to the right and left,

WHAT IT REALLY IS

splinter groups of all sizes and colorations. There is no more similarity and no less variety among those who call themselves Marxists than there is among the spectrum of those who call themselves Christians: from Eastern Orthodox to Roman Catholics, to Lutherans, Calvinists, Pentecostals, and Quakers.

The fear of monolithic Communist power and control, however, undoubtedly derives from three sources: the domineering personality of Marx and his efforts to discredit and displace competing leadership from the dominance of the Soviet Union as a highly centralized dictatorship, especially during the Stalinist period; and the numerous attempts by various national Communist rulers to use the Communist Party as a vehicle of centralized and uniform control. Although these forces have had undeniable success in generating a certain monolithic structure, especially during the Stalinist period of the 1930's and 1940's, the reality was not always as solid as the appearance. Monolithic power and control was achieved in response to internal and external crises, but (in the post-Stalin years) there has been an irresistible fragmentation process as nationalistic forces have become dominant. Paradoxically, co-operation between the Soviet Union and the Western world reached its greatest intensity during World War II when the monolithic claim was more justified.

Indeed the monolithic claim is most accurate as a description of Stalin's one-party state, concerned with "Socialism in one country" and thus departing in practice from the earlier theoretical stress on the export of revolution and the international unity of the working class. Communism is considered in terms of the one power state, under the control of Joseph Stalin. Ironically, Communism most fit its reputed image when it was least Communistic (in the sense that it was concerned with "socialism in one country" rather than exporting revolution and identifying with the international class of exploited workers). The Communists were acting primarily as Russians and nationalists attempting to overhaul their economy and resist German invasion.

Today the monolithic claim has far less justification than earlier. The indubitable fragmentation of the Communist world expresses itself in the difference among the various Communist Parties and countries, and in the decentralization of decision-making within them. There are today at least five major types of Communist states, chiefly depending on the nature of the origin of that power and its duration: Soviet Russia, with its own revolution now half a century old, a highly, though unevenly, industrialized country com-

posed of many races and languages, a super power; China, with its
own revolution now nineteen years old, with some industrialization,
but far less, and much more unevenly than, the U.S.S.R. and profoundly suspicious of the West; most of Eastern Europe, with a
Communism stemming not from indigenous revolution but resulting from Russian occupation after World War II; Yugoslavia,
where Tito made his own revolution without initial Russian support and where attempted Russian regimentation provoked a split;
and Cuba, where, unlike Eastern Europe, there was violent revolutionary seizure of power in an autocratic and semifeudal context, foreshadowed by a series of earlier revolutionary attempts, dif-
fering from China in being an island with a one-crop economy.
Thus these countries differ significantly in the age of their Communist governments, in their ideological stance, and in the kinds of
problems confronting them: population size and density, boundary
areas, degree of industrialization, possession of technological military power, racial factors, and relation to Western power.

James Reston's summary of John Kenneth Galbraith's statement
to delegates meeting in Washington to organize a National Citizens
Campaign to End the War in Vietnam bears quoting here: "Almost
all the official assumptions on which the United States entered the
war have been disproved by events. The Communist world is not
a unified menace to the free world, as we once thought, but has
fallen apart in a savage theological Sino-Soviet conflict. China
cannot even control itself, let alone control Hanoi, which has asserted its independence from Peking. The Vietcong have proved
to be more nationalist than Communist in defiance of our original
beliefs." [2]

The main fact of the Communist world after World War II has
been the Sino-Soviet split. Characteristic is a dispatch from Moscow appearing July 18, 1967, in the Philadelphia *Inquirer* emphasizing the growing division in the Communist bloc. The Soviet
Union is reported to have accused China of further isolating itself
from the rest of the Communist world by tearing up a maritime
treaty with Russia and North Korea. "The Russians issued a
diplomatic note condemning Peking's June 24 announcement that
it was dropping out of a treaty intended to save lives and help ships
and planes in distress at sea." This is merely one incident in a
series of increasingly bitter and vituperative exchanges which have
convulsed the Communist world.

Differences between the U.S.S.R. and China were replaced by

[2] *The New York Times,* July 2, 1967.

disagreement, and disagreement by antagonism, apparently beginning around 1956. The causes lay in the de-Stalinization process in
the U.S.S.R. (at a time when China felt the need for greater unity
to handle domestic problems), China's more vigorous anti-Western
stance due to Western involvement in Korea and Taiwan, Soviet
refusal to share military nuclear technology (for nationalist and
Soviet hegemony reasons), differences as to whether certain social-
economic stages could be leaped over, border disputes, and other
factors.

The East European countries have used this division and Russia's
preoccupation with its economy to develop their own national lines
of Communism. They struggle continuously for the delicate balance
between loyalty within Comecon and the Warsaw Pact and their
own national interests in opening trade, diplomatic, and cultural
relations with Western Europe. They try to follow the example of
Yugoslavia without antagonizing the U.S.S.R. The lead in this
intricate maneuvering has varied at different times, with Rumania
at the moment probably closest on the Yugoslav heels.

To Russia's dismay, a democratization process moved ahead
during 1968 in Czechoslovakia under the popular leadership of
Alexander Dubcek. Restrictions on press and public speech were
relaxed, non-Communists were added to the cabinet, and pressures
were eased on non-Communist political organizations. Fearful of
how far such liberating influence might spread, the Russians in
August 1968 moved into Czechoslovakia with Warsaw Pact troops
and quelled the reformers. This action revealed a split in the Communist world comparable to the Moscow-Peking division, for
Yugoslavia and Rumania stood on the side of the Czechs against
their invaders and every Western European Communist leader did
the same.

With greater national independence there has come a breaking
apart of the political monolith. Even some variety in election patterns is in evidence. There is also variety in the economic sphere.
China has attempted various forms of collective farms and com-
munes far beyond anything tried by the U.S.S.R. In Europe, along
with the central planning and state enterprises, some private and
co-operative enterprises have continued. There has been increasing
experimentation with variations in decentralization—in economic
planning, organization, and responsibility.

3. The third major assertion about Communism is that it is
dictatorial and largely unpopular, hence by nature opposed to
personal freedom. If one means by "dictatorial" a government that

is highly centralized, powerful, able to intervene in all of the many kinds of activity of the people living under it, and not subject to removal or alteration through a multiparty system of unmanipulated elections, then this assertion is largely true of Communist states. There are, however, growing variations, and it does not follow that a Communist government is inevitably opposed to many or all forms of personal freedom or that it must be unpopular.

The U.S.S.R. under Stalin provides the clearest illustration of these characteristics, as did the Russian-dominated governments of Eastern Europe in the 1940's and 1950's. The case of China is far more complex and unclear, although the characterization is fundamentally accurate.

Objective scrutiny of a dictatorship, whether Communist or otherwise, serves the valuable purpose of making more understandable both its strengths and its weaknesses. In this light the stereotype of dictatorial Communism breaks down into a more complicated and diverse reality.

It should be realized that most of these countries had no democratic antecedents or alternatives. The Russian Revolution was as much Russian as Marxist, with a previous history of autocracy and a reactionary Czarist government against which nothing but an equally uncompromising opposition appeared to have any chance of success. The possibilities for democratic reform in China and Cuba seemed even more unlikely; neither Chiang Kai-shek nor Batista permitted democratic reform and they governed neither with the explicit approval nor on behalf of the majority of the population. And the postrevolutionary period has not offered sufficient release from the problems of emergency pressures—of population growth, or economic needs, and foreign pressure—to encourage the development of Western-style democratic institutions. The dictatorships in Eastern Europe are best understood as the drive for Russian national security. Yet Soviet national security was not abstract and strictly interventionist. The timing of Soviet intrusion in Eastern Europe was, in part, based on the intensification of the Cold War. In 1945 the Soviet Union directly intervened in Poland and Rumania. It was not until 1947 and 1948 that it directly intervened in Bulgaria, Hungary, Czechoslovakia, and Yugoslavia. The 1968 invasion of Czechoslovakia undoubtedly stemmed in part from reasons of national security. During the crisis, *Pravda,* the official Soviet Party organ, asserted that West Germany had plans to seize East Germany and Czechoslovakia, a testimony more to a Russian phobia than the reliability of Russian military intelligence. In general, Eastern Europe serves as a buffer area to block invasion routes and guarantees allies against German invaders who had twice in this century invaded Russia, the last time at a cost of more than twenty million Russian lives.

In the second place, one must not assume that all centralized governments are equally dictatorial. There are significant differences between Stalin and post-Stalin leadership, between Tito and Hoxha. Most East Germans, even those opposed to the Socialist Unity Party government, would maintain that this government, although a dictatorship, is significantly different from, for example, the Hitler dictatorship.

Third, political systems cannot be neatly classified into either dictatorship or democracy. There are intermediate forms, and conceivably new political structures may evolve which, though not democratic in the Western sense, may be able to realize some democratic principles. Some Communist countries such as Czechoslovakia are experimenting in ways that could prove to have real democratic significance. East Germany, for example, in handling proposals for certain new fundamental laws, submits them to various forms of local community discussion that can and does culminate in amendments and modifications. The multiparty system in some Communist countries, though not independent today, may still be able to provide significant alternative points of view, or represent significant sectors of interest and needs. Loyal opposition may be able to express and organize itself in forms other than political parties, for instance, church groups, trade union organizations, or economic groupings. A continuous tension clearly exists in more industrialized Communist societies between the Party functionary, outstanding only for his uncritical loyalty, and the technocratically oriented managers, producers, and organizers. The latter appear to be quietly achieving an ever greater degree of significant decision-making power, both within and outside the Party apparatus.

In reply to Western arguments, Marxists often claim that Western-style democracy is a sham due to the lack of economic democracy. Their assertions, which contain an element of truth, are that economic inequalities negate the equality of voting power through differences in education, lobbying power, and control over mass media. Communism emphasizes economic democracy over individual liberties and political freedom, particularly since it has come to power in nations with backward peasant economies. Thus, we each define democracy in our own terms and each definition is different in the eyes of the other. The complexity of the term "democracy" and the inconsistency between rhetoric and reality has contributed to this bitter harangue and misunderstanding. In fact, the argument does not really center on democracy, although this has been the form it has assumed.

The actual practice of Western and Eastern countries shows combinations of political and economic democracy that belie the dogmatic claims of each side. We would suggest that progress in understanding and evaluating societies depends on extremely careful work in disentangling theoretical issues. Above all it is necessary to study and analyze each country's comparative progress, relative to historical conditions and disrupting conditions, in maximizing real opportunities for self-realization and mutual determination of man's collective destiny.

Related to the concept of dictatorship is the assertion that these governments are unpopular and repressive. Evidence for this is taken from the position of the Catholic Church in Poland, from Czechoslovakia, from the Hungarian Freedom Fighters, and from escapees from such countries as East Germany. To be sure, Communist countries have provided more than their share of repressive episodes: the late 1920's and 1930's in the U.S.S.R., 1953 in East Germany, 1956 in Hungary, and the peculiar struggle at the present time in China between the Maoists and the followers of Liu Shao-chi. There is a rather continuous, though not equal, suppression of certain kinds of information, and certain types of travel. One can hope that this repressive period is ending, at least in Eastern Europe, for there is considerable evidence of the gradual liberalizing of information and travel practices on the part of the U.S.S.R. and such countries as Rumania and Hungary.

The relative popularity of Communist governments with their own people is difficult to assess in the absence of elections offering significant alternatives and authentic and available public opinion surveys. Resistance leaders like Tito and Ho Chi Minh have enjoyed considerable popular support. Alexander Dubcek received overwhelming support from the Czechs when he stood up to the Russians. The Chinese Communists were also popular, at least during the early years, both because of the history of their resistance against the Japanese and because of the unpopularity of the Chiang government. Likewise in North Korea around the turn of this decade a skilled and dedicated leadership has generated such a striking economic advance that tens of thousands of Koreans were attracted from Japan to North Korea at the same time Syngman

Rhee in the South was alienating so many of his countrymen.[3] Charles Wells reported in the fall of 1967 that of 600,000 Koreans in Japan, about 200,000 of them had petitioned to migrate, many if not most of them expressing preference for *North* Korea, according to the Japanese press.[4] Other leaders and other periods could be cited to indicate considerably lower levels of popular support.

The German newspaper *Die Welt* estimated on June 19, 1965, that 3,700,000 people had left East Germany for the West, while 505,000 had moved from West to East Germany. Since the Berlin Wall was built in August 1961, over 24,000 had gone from the East at considerable danger to themselves. A variety of factors explain this phenomenon: Germany is one of the few Communist areas having a readily available alternative homeland, with the same language and even relatives for discontented elements of the population; East Germany has had to bear most of the burden of war-reparation payment to the U.S.S.R. (6,712 deutschemarks per capita as against 35 deutschemarks per capita for the West Germans, it has been estimated); East Germany has fewer raw materials, a less developed base for industrialization, little outside help, and a smaller and less skilled population with which to work; in addition to this, since this was a part of Germany that had been defeated, the Soviet Union allowed less leeway to the Ulbricht government than to other East European governments.

Not all those who left East Germany were simple lovers of freedom. There were also ex-Nazis who knew they would be jailed, young people who saw greater economic opportunity in the West, criminals who fled the police, those who sought to be reunited with their families. Except for the Jews, not many Germans fled from Nazi tyranny, and the Germans who fled from East Germany were fleeing what they viewed as foreign tyranny. Interestingly, when holiday visits were instituted for East German pensioners, only one in a thousand stayed in the West after the visit, to the surprise of both East and West German authorities.

4. The fourth characteristic ascribed to Communism, probably the most significant to the anti-Communist, is that of expansionism: that Communism exports revolution, uses military means to spread Communism, and engages in subversive activities.

Power states are tempted to expand and, throughout history, to expand without limit. This has assumed a variety of forms, whether territorial, economic, or political. Germany is a classic contem-

[3] *Encyclopedia Americana*, 1968, Vol. 16, p. 528h.
[4] *Between the Lines*, November 15, 1967.

porary case of territorial expansion because of her geographic position locked in the center of Europe and fettered by what the Nazis called "the chains of Versailles." During the nineteenth century, the main rivalries derived from European efforts to secure colonies or economic spheres of influence. In the twentieth century more subtle forms have emerged combining strategic, economic and political considerations.

Rivalry is an inevitable accompaniment to the life of nations. George F. Kennan, out of a lifetime of studying relations between the United States and the Soviet Union, reminds us:

> International life normally has in it strong competitive elements. It did not take the challenge of Communism to produce this situation. . . . There is no international relationship between sovereign states which is without its elements of antagonism, its competitive aspects. Every government is in some respects a problem for every other government, and it will always be this way so long as the sovereign state, with its supremely self-centered rationale, remains the basis of international life. . . .
>
> The result is that the relationship we have with the Soviet Union has to be compared, if we are to determine its real value, not with some nonexistent state of total harmony of interests but with what we might call the normal level of recalcitrance, of sheer orneriness and unreasonableness, which we encounter in the behavior of states anywhere, and which I am sure we often manifest in our own.[5]

As far as expansion is concerned, we Americans have known the compulsion to expand. Our whole frontier history involved this compulsion: the accretion to the United States of the entire West and Southwest and the carrying of "the white man's burden" into Central America, the Western Pacific, and the Caribbean. Nor was the method of that expansion, beginning with the near extermination of the American Indian, peculiarly humane. Whoever denounces modern Russian expansionism must also denounce American, French, Portuguese, Spanish, Dutch, and German expansionism. The British, in one of their great anthems, still sing, "Wider still and wider shall thy bounds be set; God who made thee mighty, make thee mightier yet."

Megalomania in nations—or in man—is of great current interest to the social and animal psychologists under the name of "territoriality." The brute animal limits his territory to protect himself and his mate and the satisfaction of his never-changing wants.

[5] George F. Kennan, *Russia and the West*, p. 393.

Man's power to expand his wants almost infinitely extends his territoriality accordingly; and his mobility, likewise expanding, presents him with the whole world, even with outer space, the moon, and the other planets as bases for protection against his kind. Expansionism so often appears to its possessor as nothing but defense, reflected in the attitude of Carl Sandburg's farmer's assertion that "I don't want what belongs to nobody else—I just want what jines mine." No nation makes what *it* regards as an aggressive war. We are more sophisticated, perhaps more moral, these days than were the European great powers which "carved up" Africa for their own benefit in 1881, but this, now as always, is the way a great power state acts.

Classical Marxist ideology offers only limited support for the claim that Communism expands by exporting revolution. Marx was convinced that revolution was inevitable only when and where certain conditions had been fulfilled, namely, where capitalism had developed itself within a given country to the point where all capital had accumulated in a very few hands, where these capitalists were uncontrolled by any opposing political forces, where the middle classes had disappeared, and where the proletariat had grown in size and misery. Given these conditions, one could call on the workers of the world to develop their class consciousness, to unite and throw off their chains, for they had nothing else to lose. Alternatively, in some countries, such as Holland, England, or America, where parliamentary democracy was significant, the revolution could arrive through parliamentary channels.

Lenin, interpreting capitalism in a world-wide context, argued that it could be attacked through its weakest link, that is, the exploited colonies and backward countries. This could be done by placing stress on the organized Communist Party instead of the proletariat or the peasantry as a whole; and by developing disciplined subversion of political power. But Lenin pushed his revolutionary program only in his own country, Russia. Stalin's interest was always Russia, and it was in that same Russia that, shortly after Lenin's death, the doctrine of socialism in one country became accepted dogma. Since that time the U.S.S.R. has given priority to Soviet national goals rather than the promotion of revolution abroad. Thus, George Kennan, formerly Ambassador to the Soviet Union and Chief of Policy Planning for the State Department, writes: "The image of a Stalinist Russia poised and yearning to attack the West, and deterred only by our possession of atomic weapons, was largely a creation of Western imagination, against which some of us who were familiar with Russian matters tried in vain, over the course of the years, to make our voices heard.[6]

There are far more plausible explanations for Communist expansion, especially since World War II, than the anti-Communist's vision of a sinister, subversive, monolithic monster devouring one country after another. The simplest explanation that fits the evidence is two-fold. First, in Eastern Europe, for example, Communism expanded as a result of the U.S.S.R. being on the winning side of World War II. The Russian maintenance of control over these territories may be explained by reference to Russian national interests, the recent history of two German invasions of Russia as well as previous threats from the West, such as the *cordon sanitaire,* the French threat, and the Little Entente.

In the second place, Communism of one sort or another has come to several other countries since World War II, but the subversive-expansionist view of Russian Communism is far less plausible than that of *indigenous national revolutions* arising in countries in which autocratic governments resisted needed social reforms: China, Cuba, Vietnam. The contribution of the U.S.S.R. to these revolutions was minimal. With respect to China, in both the critical 1920's and 1940's the record shows the U.S.S.R. was more interested in bolstering the Kuomintang government than in promoting Communist revolution. For a significant period in the 1920's Mao's policies were repudiated by the Soviet Union. In Cuba, Batista and Cuban conditions must be viewed as the cause of the Cuban Revolution rather than words, materiel, or personnel from the U.S.S.R.; it must be remembered that Castro was not a Communist in 1959. And in Vietnam Ho Chi Minh built a strong following of both Communists and non-Communists and a competent organization in the process of fighting for liberation from French and Japanese occupation.

The record seems to be on the whole strikingly clear; Communism does not come as a Russian or Chinese export, but rather as an aftermath of war, given certain conditions, or where indigenous revolutionary movements in stagnant societies have finally overthrown autocratic governments.

It is futile to assess the role of subversion in unstable societies, since such information is largely unobtainable. A simple count, however, indicates that subversion since World War II has most frequently been employed by right-wing or militarist groups. Such

[6] George F. Kennan, "Overdue Changes in our Foreign Policy," *Harper's Magazine,* August 1956.

coups have not aroused the concern of either the anti-Communist or the U.S. State Department.

One should neither stress nor ignore recent CIA involvements in various attempts to sabotage or overthrow existing governments —or the blundering attempts of the Chinese to foment unrest in recent years. Such evidence suggests that subversion and espionage appear, however lamentably, to be the normal weapons of national states and not anything uniquely Communist in nature.

Within the last few years, it has become fashionable to view the Russian Communists as inherently less aggressive and expansionist than the Chinese. It is said that the Chinese Communists continue to want to take over Taiwan, that they marched into Korea, that they invaded Tibet, and that they have fomented trouble on the Sino-Soviet border as well as on the Indian border. These assertions are in some sense true, yet from the standpoint of the Chinese everywhere and wartime agreements, there was no doubt of Chinese sovereignty over Taiwan. Aside from the manner in which the change in Tibet was effected, Chiang and the Kuomintang agree with Peking as to Chinese sovereignty over Tibet. The Tibetans themselves had indicated some measure of agreement by voting in the Chinese elections of 1946 and 1948.

From the point of view of the Chinese Communists the liberation of Taiwan was simply a continuation of the legitimate war against Chiang Kai-shek's group, a civil war in which the United States unilaterally intervened. They assert that they did not send volunteers into Korea until the Korean War had been going on for eight months and the United Nations (they prefer to call them United States) troops were threatening to cross the Yalu River. Furthermore, vis-a-vis the border dispute with India, they point out that the borders with the U.S.S.R. and India had been imposed by outsiders during periods of Chinese weakness, without Chinese agreement, and that it was time to regularize them. The Chinese borders with Afghanistan, Pakistan, Nepal, Burma, and Outer Mongolia have been amicably negotiated.

Many Chinese pronouncements have sounded exceedingly harsh and aggressive, to both Western and Soviet ears, but many commentators have pointed out the surprising discrepancy between their hard words and their cautious deeds, acting only when they perceive a clear threat to their country or a clear claim to territories of historic Chinese sovereignty.

It should be noted here too, since the American press tends to present Communist news selectively, that in Lin Piao's September

1965 speech—frequently quoted to show the aggressive Chinese tone—he emphasized that revolutions must be home grown.

If one does not operate by one's own efforts, does not independently ponder and solve the problems of the revolution in one's own country and does not rely on the strength of the masses, but leans wholly on foreign aid—even though this be aid from socialist countries which persist in revolution—no victory can be won, or be consolidated even if it is won.

Of course, every revolution in a country stems from the demands of its own people. Only when the people in a country are awakened, mobilized, organized and armed can they overthrow the reactionary rule of imperialism and its lackeys outside. In this sense, revolution cannot be imported.[7]

In the Western Hemisphere, Cuba furnishes a notable example of the use of revolutionary military units, under the leadership of Fidel Castro. This revolutionary force was used originally to overthrow a right-wing government that supported and benefited from free enterprise. Industry was nationalized, land reform introduced, and other measures brought an end to the free enterprise economy. American industrial and financial interests with large investments in Cuba were hurt by this action; consequently the United States suspended all relations with Cuba, tried to effect the ostracism of the Castro government by all the other nations in the two Americas, and boycotted Cuban sugar and tobacco. Castro attempted to retaliate as best he could, and from the days when this nonideological revolutionist overthrew Batista, he has moved steadily, in reaction to American pressure, toward Communist alliance and Communist ideology. Yet the form of the alliance is tenuous, as Castro, despite Cuban dependence on Soviet economic aid and military help, has sustained a national and independent line. This independence is best reflected in Castro's recent berating of Latin-American Communist Parties for their nonrevolutionary stance, as well as in the jailing in early 1966 of a prominent Moscow-oriented Communist.

He did succeed in securing Soviet missiles in 1962, but in the "eyeball-to-eyeball" confrontation between Khrushchev and Kennedy, the Russians yielded and the missiles were withdrawn. Castro makes continuous efforts to encourage guerrilla activity in Latin-American countries, with questionable success, yet it is more the example of his regime in Cuba that encourages Latin Americans to

[7] *Peking Review,* No. 32, August 4, 1967, pp. 26 and 33.

replace archaic, autocratic systems than it is the work of Castroite agents.

The most relevant contemporary expression of frantic anti-Communism is the domino theory, which dominates our official policy toward Vietnam; if South Vietnam falls, all other Asian countries are fated to follow; their will and capacity to resist would atrophy; as Vietnam goes, so goes Asia! All of it.

The fear of Communism expressed in the domino theory is no new phenomenon. At the time of the Russian Revolution, Churchill feared that all of Europe and the colonies would tumble before the Communist menace. Fifty years afterward, the majority of the dominoes in Europe still stand. Cuba became Communist in 1959. If the domino theory had validity, then Castro-type revolutions would have swept South America. There has not been one.

The domino theory does have this to be said for it: Every national and international event has its repercussions and influences other events. And a victory for nationalism in Vietnam would hearten other nationalists elsewhere, just as a victory for the democratization process in Czechoslovakia would have encouraged moderating influences in the Eastern European countries. The tragedy of the American misreading of Vietnam is that we have thwarted the aspirations of the people for true independence and have lent our support to oppressive dictatorships like those of Diem and Ky and Thieu.

Perhaps the anti-Communist's avowed fear is not of Communist aggressiveness and expansionism but the process of change itself. Perhaps he does not fear clear military or violent revolutionary activity in other countries so much as he fears changes in the American status quo in the direction of socialism. Thus, he promotes his conservatism with respect to the American scene by appealing to the popularly accepted fear that Communism (or socialism, for they seem to mean the same thing to him) is taking over the world by illegitimate and illegal means. But Communist and socialist movements must be analyzed separately.

5. One further assertion is characteristically made by the anti-Communists about the Communists: that they are atheistic and immoral. Indeed, the two words are used as synonyms by anti-Communists, although they are not. The atheist can be moral, and the believer in God can be quite immoral in his behavior.

The basis of this stereotype does not lie in the average American's personal experience of Communists. Very few American people, indeed, know any Communists personally, accepting them as do people in most other parts of the world as human beings and acquaintances. Communism thus becomes everything evil, sinister, and Machiavellian, and the less-than-human Communists are everything suspicious, devious, ruthless, unethical, and dishonest—just because we know *of* them, but do not *know* them.

Interestingly, our main perception of Communism is that offered by individual ex-Communists. We tend uncritically to accept their reports and testimonials, ignoring the bitterness of their break and the circumstances of their recantation and not questioning the vituperation and alienation that surround their rejection of Communism. We are impressed by their stories of intrigue and power.

It would be very difficult to show that Communist individuals or countries are any more, or less, moral than non-Communist individuals or countries. Generally speaking there is about the same range and distribution of immoralities in the sense of breaking of promises and treaties, justifying vicious or unfair policies as means to remote but noble ends, or treating certain groups of humans as expendable in order to achieve a world of peace and order. Most nations break treaties when it is in their self-interest to do so, and morality, in the usual sense of the word, plays a minor part in diplomatic decisions. George F. Kennan, commenting on some of Russia's more reprehensible acts, once observed, "This is all too similar to the way other great powers have behaved and still behave. The differences are relative." [8]

A person with experience in both the Communist and the capitalist world might observe a somewhat more compromisingly pragmatic accommodation to the materialist nature of man in capitalistic society, and a rather more idealistic, optimistic, even righteously crusading attitude—occasionally one-sided and fanatic—among the Communists. There is a certain impressive bright-eyed moral attitude of condemnation among convinced Communists toward bourgeois vices such as gambling, prostitution, nonproductivity, and imperialist exploitation that is very suggestive of Calvinist attitudes of an earlier day.

If there is a difference, it probably is that a Communist would justify an immorality in the name of a group, a class, or a country, or for historical progress, but seldom on behalf of himself as an individual. The non-Communist, on the other hand, would justify immorality either on behalf of a group or for himself.

Undoubtedly Communism is in some sense atheistic, although

[8] George F. Kennan, "Overdue Changes in our Foreign Policy," *Harper's Magazine*, August 1956.

this same attitude could be better and more accurately described in other words. Part of this attitude is traceable to the philosophical materialism of Marx, but it should be noticed that this is not materialism, in a popular sense, having no connection with either the pursuit of worldly wealth or with morality. Philosophically it should not be confused with mechanistic materialism for it does not assert that mind, or spirit, or life is merely matter. Rather in being dialectical the Marxist can admit to whatever degree he wishes to what a non-Marxist would call spiritual or vital, for matter evolves through various levels. For some Marxists, to be a materialist is equivalent to saying that most human decisions are essentially caused by economic factors, an assertion with which many Western-ers would agree.

Finally, for both Marx and many contemporary Marxists, this same materialism represents a kind of prophetic condemnation of a church and religion that lost its spiritual idealism as it concen-trated upon temporal power and advantages. The biting edge of truth in this heretical condemnation of orthodoxy gone covetous should no more be lost upon those of us who call ourselves religious and Christian, than should the similar condemnation by Savonarola or Luther or Calvin of a worldly Roman Catholicism, or by Spinoza of a Judaism gone mundane, or by Buddha of a degenerating Hin-duism.

Admittedly the Soviet Union has an official antichurch policy, and there have been repressive campaigns against Jews and against the Eastern Orthodox Church. Likewise in China and in Eastern Europe, there have been programs of condemnation, harassment, and even repression of churches as well as of public expression of religious belief.

However, there is truth in the counterclaim made by some Chinese Christians that the Communists are not trying to kill Christianity but trying to prove that the substance of Christianity is not identical with Western bourgeois forms of Christianity. There is also truth in the claim that in Europe the movement is not against freedom of worship and religious belief, as such, so much as against a church that has assumed temporal and political power; Com-munism in part wishes to accomplish the same separation of church and state that was accomplished after 1688 in England, the United States, and France. Although the struggle between church and state in Communist Poland, with its 90 per cent Catholic population, has been particularly bitter, in most other Communist countries an acute church-state struggle seems to be a thing of the past, replaced by limited forms of state-religious co-operation or limited forms of administrative harassment. A number of Communist countries have lamentably found no better way than prison for the Jehovah's Witnesses, who have also found their way in significant numbers to prison cells in the West. East Germany, moreover, has become the first Communist government to recognize, even if in a very limited way, the right to exemption from military duty for religious conscientious objectors.

The Anti-Communist's View of Himself

The anti-Communist's view of himself is as distorted as his view of Communism. Whereas he sees the Communist as the personification of all that is evil, he sees himself as an angel of light.

Again the reality is more complex than the myth.

It is very consoling to view ourselves as models of rectitude, even more so as misunderstood models of rectitude. Simple honesty, however, compels us to look at ourselves in the same way as we would look at the Communist, both empathetically from the inside and realistically from the outside. Only in this way can we make rational assessments and recommend reasonable courses of action.

Dwight Morrow observed once that we Americans are prone to judge other nations by their actions and our own by its ideals. To see oneself as a model of rectitude is a phenomenon not confined to any one culture, or only to cultures. That is a personal inclination too. It may be, in part, a salutary psychological mechanism calculated to develop confidence in one's own being and activities. It may be due to the fact that when we view ourselves we see both our actions and intentions, whereas when we observe another we see only his actions and never his intentions. Given all this, semantics comes to our aid. We brighten our own behavior by describing it in glowing euphemisms. The same actions when performed by someone whose intentions we don't know or don't trust are deprecated by us. Thus the conjugation: I am persevering; you are stubborn; he is a pig-headed fool.

A further consideration is the selectivity of information gathering, especially in a day of mass media. Information from close to home covers the full spectrum of events with emotional coloration from good to bad; but information from far away is usually newsworthy only when it is catastrophic or frightening. The undramatic, constructive, slowly developing good elements of human and social life are not sensational and attract less attention than the negative aspects of life. This selectivity is a prominent feature in Communist publications as it is in our own.

Our double standard of judgment is revealed when we look at Vietnam. The Russians and the Chinese support one faction. They came in response to appeals from that group. We support another faction in answer to their appeals. The kinds of actions are very similar except that we send personnel as well as materiel, and they ship mainly materiel. But our actions are defensive and peaceful; theirs are aggressive. They commit atrocities, but we only admit civilian casualties to the hospital. They don't believe in coexistence because they believe in wars of national liberation, but our war to liberate their nation from Communism is to free them from tyranny. When we offer negotiations with one hand and increase the bombing with the other, that is not deceit but a diplomatic move to put pressure on them to come to the peace table; but if they were to do the same, it would be trickery.

If it were profitable, a long list could be made of the lack of American rectitude as measured by the breaking of agreements. We signed the Kellogg-Briand Pact in 1928, renouncing war, but committed aggression within its definition of aggression more than a dozen times during the next decade. We invaded Nicaragua, but excused our action as defensible under the Monroe Doctrine. We joined with the Organization of American States in agreeing not to interfere in the domestic affairs of American states, and then sent troops to the Dominican Republic in 1965.

We signed the Potsdam Agreement to break up German corporations and make German militarism impossible, and proceeded to violate it without any excuse, except the Russians were doing likewise. We committed the Japanese to a constitution guaranteeing a nonmilitary status, and are now pressuring for a change. We held on to Guam and Okinawa after World War II was over, but refuse to equate this with Russia's holding on to war-gained territory.

Such references are enough to indicate that our behavior is less than morally perfect. We play the game of national and bloc interest as well as other countries do.

The supposed pluralism of the anti-Communist's world is severely limited. He fails to see the pluralism in the Communist world just as he fails to see the limited nature of pluralism in his own world. He requires of his allies, as individuals and as countries, not that they choose their own way, whatever the outcome may be; they must choose to be non-Communists. When possible, he goes farther and requires that they be as anti-Communist as he. A fellow countryman is not quite patriotic if he does not avow his anti-Communism. If he does not confess to it freely, then he should be compelled to sign loyalty oaths and Communist disclaimers, just as he should avoid those groups listed as subversive by the Attorney General.

To the anti-Communist a "Socialist" is suspect and a "progressive" is part of a "front" for Communism. Association or peaceful relations with Communists becomes an act of betrayal or at least of self-deception. The fellow traveler, knowingly or naïvely, furthers the Communist's cause by shielding him or even by agreeing with him on as much as a single issue, even if for quite different reasons. The word "Communist" becomes a club with which to attack all that one dislikes, certainly all those who advocate any change in the status quo: civil rights, fair employment practices, Medicare, any extension of government services or spending (*except* for defense). Because of the powerful and insidious nature of Communism no amount of overkill is too great, and because Communists aren't quite human, weapons of the most cruelly destructive potency can be justified. Because of the threat, no objections can be made to billions for military expenses. Welfare programs, subsidies, and poverty programs however are resisted as detracting from the vital business of erecting a colossal military apparatus against Communism. Besides, welfarism is regarded by anti-Communists as disguised, incipient Communism.

In the anti-Communist crusade, Birchers, Klansmen, and ultra-conservative churchmen find some wealthy businessmen a lucrative source of financial and political support. These supporters promote greater military spending while opposing domestic programs of any sort that are left of center.

In foreign policy, self-determination seems to mean political forms and candidates that are at least non- and preferably anti-Communist. If the Vietnam elections promised by the Geneva Agreement in 1954 might result in the election of a Ho Chi Minh, then they should not be held. It will be recalled that President Eisenhower wrote, "I have never talked or corresponded with a person knowledgeable in Indochinese affairs who did not agree that had the elections been held as of the time of the fighting [1954], possibly 80 per cent of the population would have voted for Communist Ho Chi Minh as their leader." [9] The so-called "free elec-

---

[9] Dwight D. Eisenhower, *Mandate for Change, 1953–1956: The White House Years*, p. 372.

tions" in Vietnam in 1967 were a farce before they began. All Communist, neutralist, and known peace candidates were excluded. Any candidate capable of commanding a popular following was prevented from running. Rigid restrictions were imposed on campaigning, irregularities abounded, and the majority of the Vietnamese did not even participate. Yet the election was presented to the American public as free and democratic.

Since Chiang is anti-Chinese-Communist, we do not insist on free elections for Taiwan Chinese, or for the five times more numerous native Taiwanese who have been virtually forgotten. If a revolution is leftist, as in Cuba, we do everything we can to starve or boycott it out of existence, but if a right-wing military coup is successful, as in Brazil, we extend it diplomatic recognition overnight. The logic of this anti-Communist policy does not allow for international pluralism to fit the different needs and conditions of different countries, but asks only the one question, "Is it anti-Communist?" If the answer is in the affirmative, then aid and help are forthcoming. With countries that wish to be nonaligned or neutral we are honestly puzzled, and we find it hard to relate ourselves to them.

Some of our closest international allies have the same dictatorial, freedom-suppressing, antiliberal characteristics that we profess to dislike in Communist governments. Since the American anti-Communist apparently believes that people in all other countries, including the underdeveloped ones, enjoy adequate standards of living, a measure of personal security, and political freedom, he consequently assumes that every revolution threatens peace, comfort, and freedom. The sad fact, however, is that for the vast majority of the impoverished people of underdeveloped countries there is no peace, comfort, security, or freedom. A revolution, Communist or otherwise, may well look like the way out of their distressing situation. To these people the expression "free world" is a mockery; self-determination is something that others enjoy; and the immorality of the unlimited use of power is a part of their daily existence. So expressions such as imperialism and exploitation have meaning for them, though little for us.

Is it true that we are generous? Yes, probably more so than any other nation in the history of the world, as measured by the outflow of foreign aid, Marshall Plan, and Point Four programs. All of this is praiseworthy.

The objective of these policies, however, was not simple altruism. Our purpose in ceding economic or military aims was to achieve a world order that was consistent with our objectives. It was not simple support for self-determination or economic development. If this can be defended in national interest terms, this is not the same as internationalism and moral altruism. It is also true, by the same criteria, that Communist countries are likewise generous in proportion to their lesser wealth.

Are we peaceful? Yes, if by peace we mean peace and order on our terms; but then we must allow that Communist countries are also peaceful on their terms. But we are also a great warfare state as well. We supply weapons to Pakistan and India for use against China, and are disgusted when they use them against each other. We build the military power of one South American state, and then must help another South American state with weapons to maintain the balance. We sell arms to Israel, and we also peddle them to the Arab states. We insist that West Germany maintain an army of half a million men, and locate nuclear weapons on its soil. We try to hold a tight military alliance in NATO, long after most other NATO countries are convinced the Russian military threat has subsided.

We station American troops around the world, and maintain a peacetime draft at home. We send American fighting men to Korea, and push the UN into following us there, while sending American naval power to the Straits of Taiwan without UN support. We send American advisers to Vietnam, and end by fighting that undeclared war with our troops more engaged than those of the Vietnamese. Meanwhile we increase the American military presence in Thailand, and bomb Laos and North Vietnam from Thai airfields.

Paradoxically, we also supply the Communists with some of their weapons. In Vietnam, Americans have been shot with guns "made in U.S.A." In China on the first May Day celebration after the Communist conquest of the mainland, there was a day long parade in Peking of men, tanks, guns, and all manner of weapons. At the end of it Mao is said to have declared, "All this is thanks to the Americans." They were captured from, bought from, or brought over by defecting and defeated Kuomintang troops.

Yes, we are peace-loving, but we also find it expedient to wage war and to support war measures. Historian Henry Steele Commager's words in the July 16, 1967, *New York Times Book Review* might lead us to believe that we are in fact even outdoing the Communists. "Now," he writes, "we have military installations in some thirty countries, a CIA operating in twice that number, and we are waging war six thousand miles away to stop what we consider 'aggression.' We have moved from limited isolation to unlimited intervention more rapidly than any other nation in history, and more ambitiously, too. We are today the leading imperial power in the world, the leading military power, the leading interventionist power, with commitments even more extensive than our engagements. . . ."

Most of our fellow citizens are convinced that Communism threatens our freedom and our way of life. In a very real sense this is true, since the Communist nations like most other people are propelled by nationalist aspirations, and wherever these clash with our nationalist aspirations they pose a threat to us. Again, perspective is of the utmost importance, and the ability to see clearly that even as the Communists threaten our freedom and way of life, so we constitute a giant threat to theirs.

We must recall that in 1918 we joined with other Allied Powers at the close of World War I to invade Russia in an effort to stop Bolshevism. With the ending of World War II in 1945, we turned a very cold shoulder toward our erstwhile ally, terminating lend-lease assistance immediately, while a request from the Soviet Union for a loan to assist in carrying on reconstruction out of the devastation of war was conveniently "lost" in the files of the State Department. And some students of history and political analysts assert that the atom bombs were primarily intended to impress the Russians with the fearsomeness of American power since the Japanese already had sent out peace feelers prior to Hiroshima. NATO may be a defensive alliance from our point of view, but it has always appeared threatening to the Communist world. Even more so since the inclusion of West Germany, whose rearming the Soviets regard with the utmost dread and fear.

China's experience has been similar to that of the Soviet Union. In the early 1950's it was only when American troops came dangerously close to the Chinese border in North Korea that the Chinese retaliated by sending their own troops into battle. Our Seventh Fleet has patrolled the waters of the Taiwan Straits for the past two decades, our planes repeatedly violate Chinese air space, and now we are waging a bloody war close to the Chinese border in Vietnam. Unrecognized as a nation, excluded from the United Nations, it is small wonder that the Chinese feel threatened by America.

Yes, Communist countries do pose a threat to our freedom and way of life, even more so as Russia perfects her nuclear arsenal and China explodes a hydrogen bomb, but to an even greater extent, because of our greater military might and access to bases and positions closer to their soil, we pose a more terrifying threat to the Communist nations.

We see the world through American eyes with American assumptions, convinced that our intentions are honorable and our concerns altruistic. The world, especially the underdeveloped countries, looks at the United States through the jaundiced eyes of disease, undernourishment, and personal insecurity, and to these eyes the American presence appears as unattainable wealth, as mechanical and military power, as napalm and nuclear weapons of destruction. To many people in many countries American help is to be feared at least as much as Chinese or Russian help. They seem to be caught with their frustrated hopes between the Scylla of Communism and the Charybdis of anti-Communism, both serving primary goals that may be irrelevant, if not exacerbating, to their own problems.

Henry Steele Commager's review of Ronald Steel's *Pax Americana* in the July 16, 1967, *New York Times Book Review* summarized our contention that anti-Communism's conviction about the benevolence of American intentions is not shared by the rest of the world:

At the close of the war [World War II] we had stood at the pinnacle of power and prestige. We set up NATO to protect Western Europe, the OAS to organize common enterprises in the Western Hemisphere, SEATO to maintain peace in the Far East. Now, twenty years later, NATO is bankrupt, the OAS is in disarray, SEATO a bad joke. The grand alliance is gone and we find ourselves without a really firm friend among any of our former associates, supported only by the puppet governments in South Korea, Taiwan, and Thailand. Regarding ourselves as the champion of freedom and the paladin of peace, we find ourselves regarded by most of the nations of the globe as the leading military and imperialist power of the Western World.

The Anti-Communist's View of His Own Effectiveness

Given the anti-Communist's oversimplified view, with the good on one side and the bad on the other, he believes that he must exterminate the evil, or at least prevent its spread. His identification of evil with Communists or dupes of Communists allows him to concentrate all his moral idealism on this one crusade: one more evil to eliminate, and mankind will have reached the end of his troubles. For the anti-Communist, the defeat of Communism means the end of unrest and anxiety. Since this is the case, one must deal harshly with these fomenters of trouble. The use of subversion and the use of all military power including napalm and, if necessary, the whole arsenal of atomic, bacterial, and chemical weapons, is justifiable. Having thus justified a hard line policy, the anti-Communist is free to be flexible only about rollback, containment, or combat, depending upon the circumstances. The anti-Communist convinces himself that it is our deterrent power alone that has arrested the spread of Communism and now causes dissension within its ranks.

The truth again is more complicated. If our military strength has restrained the Soviet Union in certain crimes, still our deterrent power has also generated the tensions and the military threat that we fear. The show of military power by one nation stimulates the desire for greater power on the part of another. The manufacture of missiles by the United States provokes the manufacture of missiles by the Soviet Union, and in the end no one is more secure. Indeed everyone is less secure, even though more protected.

It is not only responsible American leadership that has learned to be in awe of the incredible nuclear destructive power now available. Linus Pauling estimates that, compared to the six megatons expended over six years by all involved powers during World War II there now exist (1966) some 320,000 megatons of weapons, sufficient to maintain a World War II type war every day for 146 years.[10] Soviet leadership, at least since Khrushchev, has apparently recognized the new dimension in world relations, for one of the key four pillars of his co-existence policy was that neither Communist nor capitalist countries could any more hope to destroy the other system, since any victory would have to be mutually destructive. There might be some anti-Communist satisfaction in exterminating the people of Russia, but it would be an empty satisfaction because we would not be here to enjoy it.

In the second place, the conclusion that our deterrence deters is true only if the assumption of anti-Communism is right and Communist governments are inherently out to overthrow all non-Communist governments. This insurrectionary policy is neither so dominant nor so universal as the anti-Communist would have us believe. Moreover, much Russian expansionism can be more plausibly interpreted as protection of their western flank against a recurrence of German invasion; much Chinese expansionism can be more plausibly interpreted as clarifying their sovereignty and delin-

---

[10] Linus Pauling, in his introduction to Sidney Lens, *The Futile Crusade: Anti-Communism as American Credo,* p. 7.

eating the borders of territories with some claim to being called
Chinese. Strange as it may seem, nationalism has exerted a stronger
claim on developing Communist countries than international worker
solidarity and the class war. China might well be viewed as trying
to achieve an Asian version of the Monroe Doctrine. Furthermore,
astute China watchers have begun to recognize a peculiar semantic
function in hostile Chinese pronouncements. They employ what
has been called verbal deterrence intended not only to intimidate
their enemies but to goad the Chinese themselves into greater zeal
in tackling domestic problems.

INTERPLAY BETWEEN THE COMMUNIST AND
THE CAPITALIST WORLD

Anti-Communism sees the negative characteristics of Communism as fixed and permanent features, inexplicable and ineradica-
ble traits of Communist character. However, a more adequate analysis would see these traits as largely determined by conditions, as
reactions to various kinds of perceived stimuli. To the degree that
this is true, so-called Communist aggressiveness then is not a fixed
and permanent structure, but a modifiable response. The causes of
Communist aggressiveness may be found in the urgency of the
constructive tasks they want to accomplish, in intransigent resistance by others to the accomplishment of these tasks, and in the
threats to the existence of their system. One of the contributing
causes to Communist aggressiveness, where it exists, is the very
attitude and policy of the anti-Communist nations.

From Karl Marx until the present day, Communists have seen
capitalism as a deterministically evolving structure, doomed by its
own inherent defects and unable to modify or reform its early
harshness toward the working class. The only reasonable Communist alternative was a revolutionary approach. Marx was wrong,
and capitalism, accompanied by political democracy, has been able
to reform itself significantly. Communist systems that were fostered
on this false premise, however, have found a kind of vindication
in those precapitalist societies most resistant to social and political
reform. Confirmation of the Communist myth was further enhanced
when the capitalist countries did everything they could to frustrate
the furtherance of Communist revolutions in such countries as
Russia and China which are now Communist.

From the beginnings of the Russian Revolution, the Western
powers have provided Communists with evidence that Communism

could develop peacefully only when capitalism has changed its character, which according to Communist theory it could not do. The leadership in this anti-Communist crusade was not originally carried by the United States, but since World War II the United States has assumed that obligation. From 1918 to 1920, fourteen foreign armies occupied parts of the U.S.S.R. The United States, not recognizing the Soviet Union until 1933, has shown a consistent antagonism moderated only during World War II and the last few years. The People's Republic of China, with enormous, urgent domestic tasks to accomplish and with a leadership eager to accomplish those tasks, has been boycotted, ostracized, militarily surrounded, and even its civil war unceremoniously and unilaterally interfered in by the United States. Much the same description fits Castro's Cuba.

Under these circumstances there has been a strong temptation to resist, to fight back, to destroy that which threatens them. The so-called Chinese paranoia, its persecution complex, has ample explanation. The failure of other countries, the U.S.S.R. included since 1959, to help China significantly has been interpreted by the Chinese as a constant military and political threat to their continued existence. That they have been as restrained in their actions as they have is more surprising than that they have been hostile. That restraint may have been the result of military weakness and, if so, with the rapid development of Chinese nuclear capability, time may be running out for befriending China.

Not that foreign opposition has singlehandedly caused Communist intransigence, but rather each side, feeling threatened, has developed policies that promote the same policies of intransigence on the other side. Aggressiveness begets aggressiveness; toughness begets toughness; hostility, hostility. It might be otherwise if some of the opponents were small, weak, and isolatable. These might be browbeaten into unwilling submissiveness. But neither the interrelated Western world nor the Communist world can be isolated and coerced into pleasantness. We have to accept each other because we must.

There is reason not only to believe that we must live with each other, but to hope that we can. For just as negative attitudes and negative policies tend to generate the same kind of attitudes and policies on the other side, so too friendliness, co-operation, the removal of threat and hostility, willingness to negotiate differences, if persisted in wisely, realistically, and as long-range policy, tend to promote those same attitudes and policies on the other side.

The failure of the hard-line policy can be demonstrated through the history of the Cold War. The world was brought to the brink of disaster several times and yet neither side could force, externally, changes upon the other side. Finally both sides had to admit the failure of Cold War policies in a stalemate of hostility. In that process, the West must share the blame with the Communist world. With respect to Germany, for example, after a year or two of Russian political initiatives, it was the West that first adopted those unilateral measures that the East later emulated: separate currency zones, remilitarization of partial German zones, separate political sovereignty. The outcome was a partitioned and polarized Germany, each side armed, hostile, and linked into separate economic and military systems.

It is imperative to develop and extend the emerging East-West *détente,* and East and West co-operation, without further North-South polarization or Oriental-Occidental polarization. Before responsive processes can generate co-operation and competitive co-existence, anti-Communism, as a mode of oversimplified thought, must be eliminated. The direct responsibility for this lies with us. We must delineate a more hopeful and constructive set of attitudes and doctrines of man than those expressed in anti-Communism.

DOCTRINE OF MAN

A humanistic, empirical, and morally sensitive doctrine of man is needed as an alternative to any form of anti- ideology. Perhaps even more important than changes in institutions or changes in policies is a change in attitude and perspective. If an adequate set of attitudes—a new spirit—can be achieved, the appropriate institutions and policies will rapidly recommend themselves. Before we turn, in the final chapter, to concrete proposals for action, let us consider first here an alternative kind of attitude to anti-Communism, one that is contemporary, though of ancient lineage, one that is tough-minded in its empiricism and realism, yet creative and hopeful in its analysis of how to confront Communism.

If our analysis is substantially correct, then it is clear that anti-Communism commits a three-fold error: (1) it maximizes the evil and minimizes the good in the Communist; (2) it maximizes the good and minimizes the evil in himself; and (3) it relies on hatred and violence as the means of combating the evil seen exclusively in the Communist.

We do not recommend as an alternative ignoring either the negative aspects of Communism or the positive virtues on our side. We assume that these will be seen. There is no danger—given human nature—that they won't be. What must be seen, if we are to avoid disaster, is the beam in our eye as well as the mote in the Communist's. Seeing ourselves through the eyes of others is a healthy antidote to overly euphemistic self-perception. We must see the strong points in Communism as clearly and charitably as we see our own. And we must realize that the methods of hatred and violence are today as anachronistic in the relations of nations as they were yesterday in the relations of individuals.

The crux of this new perspective is given in the title of William Barton's Swarthmore Lecture for 1966, "The Moral Challenge of Communism." It is not so much the political and military challenge that we need to respect, as the moral challenge. Indeed the overemphasis by anti-Communism on the political and military challenge blinds us to that more significant challenge.

Barton does not fail to list some negative ethical aspects of Marxist-Leninist society: insufficient attention to the uniqueness and value of the individual as an end in himself; the failure to appreciate the profound moral effect spiritual experience can have on an individual's way of life; a disturbing self-confidence in men's power to effect moral improvement through environmental changes; an unwillingness to learn from non-Communists; and the subordination of moral values to political criteria. (Note how these same charges can be applied to the anti-Communist!) But Barton gives full weight to other Communist qualities that are usually underestimated: the desire to apply moral principles to the entire social environment; the emphasis on implementing theory in practice; massive social improvements; campaigns against antisocial behavior; and the value of the concept of equals working together in community.

Let us take a fresh look at Communism, and at ourselves, and at our responses to Communism.

If the anti-Communist does not know what it is that he is anti-, his chance of opposing it successfully is no better than the blind bowman's. But the characteristic fact of American life is that an understanding of Communism—or even an interest in understanding it—is in inverse proportion to the ardor to strike out against it. There is nothing peculiarly American about this phenomenon; the mind of man runs to simplification, and the more complex the problem, the fewer there are who have the patience to analyze it while all around them cry out that we must fight or perish.

But Communism is not a simple concept with one immediately apprehensible definition. It has three entirely separable—if miscible —meanings. It is, first, a theory (and practice) of the production and distribution of material goods. It is, second, a world revolution in our time whose historical power seat is Moscow (with Peking disputing the point). It is, third, two great power states, the Union of Soviet Socialist Republics and Communist China, involved in a world power struggle with the world's other great power state, the United States (the struggle for the world between the United States and Russia was specifically predicted in 1835 by Alexis de Tocqueville, who had never heard of the then 17-year-old Karl Marx).

The Soviet Union and the United States are the two great power states that the end of World War II left face to face and alone in the world *without respect to ideology*. As China emerges, the balance of this confrontation will be altered in a manner still unpredictable. Historically the division of the world, that is, the known and accessible world, has been into two power-state blocs and has always involved an armaments race ending in war.

A significant footnote is indicated here. It has not hitherto been of the essence of this division that one party consider its civilization superior to the other, although the view that *we* are civilized and *they* are savage gains invariable currency in the course of conflict. (To the ancient Greeks the word *barbaros,* meaning "stranger," was not as pejorative as it is to us.) But the Americans have traditionally looked upon Russia as outer darkness; if, said Abraham Lincoln, he could bring himself to accept racism, he would prefer to live in Russia, where autocracy was to be found pure and unalloyed by the pretense of liberty. There has never been any substantial emigration from Russia to America. Few Americans ever went to Russia. Few Americans over the centuries have ever seen a Russian.

The second meaning of Communism, in our time, is world revolution. We Americans ought to know what revolution—and world revolution—means. We are all sons and daughters of the world revolution that proclaimed all men, not all Americans, or all Englishmen, or all white men, but *all men* are created equal. We are all sons and daughters too, of the Judaeo-Christian revolution that proclaimed the One God and the redemption of man through his only begotten Son. Christ was not a national revolutionary. His was not a war of national liberation. His universal love was meant to overcome the whole world.

Now whoever, with such certainty as men may have, believes that he has hold of a doctrine which is the only right doctrine and the only just doctrine, and cares for his fellowman, and finds himself in a society which subscribes to another doctrine, must be a revolutionary, whether he uses violent or nonviolent methods, and must try in good conscience to extend what he regards as the benefits of his right and just doctrine to all men everywhere. If the Methodists or the Baptists or the Presbyterians or the Congregationalists are satisfied that there is only one way to be saved and that way theirs, they, like the Holy Office of the Roman Catholic Inquisition, would be derelict in their duty to God and man if they did not go to considerable pains to convert the heathen and use the most persuasive means they could command to repulse the infidels and discourage backsliders among their communicants.

Revolution is, and makes, its own law. Its business is the overturn of the established order maintained by the order's laws. Revolutions are not democratic in the accepted sense. They are not voted into power within the prevailing framework. The American Revolution, too, was the work of a minority that had enough fervor to rebel, and as the Whites fled from the Reds in Russia, so the Loyalists fled from the Rebels of 1776. But the condition of revolutionary success is the willingness of the populace as a whole to see the old order overthrown. The Bolsheviks could not have held power for a week if the Russian people as a whole had been *against* them.

Forgetting our own experience, and unschooled in that of others, we like to believe that a revolution is the work of a few (or a few thousand) masters of deceit who, until they strike, have operated as a secret conspiracy against the liberty and property of a whole people, unwarned, unprepared, and therefore helpless to resist their subjection to an evil regime.

Thus we forget (if we ever bothered to know it) that the Nazis polled 37 per cent of the votes in the German election of 1932. Their plurality, under the European parliamentary system, entitled them to come to power; and they came to power (as Hitler never wearied of boasting) legally, with much more popular support, indeed, than the Democrats have had in Mississippi. But the revolution picks up the power in the streets, the power lost, one way or another, by the established order before the revolution occurs. Thus the Russian housewives—prior to the overthrow of the Czar in 1917—went into the streets clamoring for bread, and the mutinous soldiers refused to disperse them. Christ, the Revolutionary, was crucified according to established custom among the law-abiding and law-preserving Romans.

Our own American Revolution is a record of horrors—though a comparatively mild one, and in part because the defenders of the established order were unable to get at the revolutionaries. But whoever supposes that the Russian Communists invented the torment of their ideological enemies ought to read MacKinlay Kantor's *Andersonville*, the story of a Confederate prison in the Civil War.

Nobody can read Marx without feeling the fervor that moved the man to seek to improve the lot of mankind, without sensing his implacable anger at the exploitation, indeed, the murder of five-year-olds, at the hands of an irresponsible capitalism. Marx scouted the possibility of reform. In despair he became a revolutionary. He was wrong in many decisive respects. But he stands, still, a monument to the hopes of men for a betterment of their worldly condition and a terrible challenge to a world which professes, in Christian charity, the love of one's neighbor as oneself. Out of that love, to which that German atheist sacrificed all worldly advancement for himself, came all the horrors of Stalinism; no more fatal an error can be made than the ascription of those horrors to the doctrines of Communism.

The revolutions that in our time convulse the world are of many kinds. But they have one condition, and one operative principle, in common: That condition is economic poverty, bordering on starvation, among two thirds of the world's people, while a minority live in luxury. The people of the United States, not through their wickedness, nor yet through their virtue, but through historical and geographical accident, comprising some 7 per cent of the world's population, enjoy some 50 per cent of its income. "Every city," said Plato, two thousand years ago, "is two cities, a city of the many poor and a city of the few rich; and these two cities are always at war." In this situation we Americans are always at war. In this situation we Americans are inevitably cast as counterrevolutionary.

So the religious American finds himself in tension. His affluence disposes him to defend his advantages against a disadvantaged world, but his faith renders him sensitive to their plight. His faith should make him a nonviolent revolutionary eager to see the world's deprivation brought to an end.

The one operative principle to be found in the revolutions of our time is the social ownership of the means of production and distribution. This is the third meaning of Communism. But it is not confined to Marxist Communism, or even to Communism. It is the operative principle of many other forms of social organization. The late Prime Minister Shastri of India said at his inauguration, "Our objective is socialism." The American farmer with his privately owned machinery, most of which stands unused most of the time, does not need to overexert his imagination to understand that *some sort* of common ownership of such machinery is the only hope of agriculture in underdeveloped countries without the private means of capital investment. He adopts the same socialist principle in his thousands of co-operatives.

Marx overlooked the attendant *political* disadvantage of social ownership vested directly or indirectly in government, just as we overlook the *economic* disadvantage of private ownership in an impoverished society. "Whose bread I eat, his song I sing." Economic control carries the threat, especially under the monopoly conditions of state Communism, of political dictatorship. But economic liberty in a poor society carries the still more desperate threat of starvation. They who have lived under both kinds of tyranny— hunger *and* dictatorship—seem to prefer the latter to the former. We who have lived under neither are poorly qualified to argue their preference to be Red rather than dead.

For those Americans who hope to stop Communism in Vietnam, the most dreadful report ever emanating from the wretched and bleeding country is not a report of battles lost to the Vietcong, or of continued infiltration in spite of the stupendous bombing of the North. It is a report published September 2, 1965, in *The New York Times* under the name of the distinguished associate editor of that newspaper, James Reston. Writing from Saigon, Mr. Reston said: "Premier Nguyen Cao Ky told this reporter Tuesday that the Communists were closer to the people's yearnings for social justice and an independent national life than his own government." In another sense it is the assertion by an American major justifying the destruction through American air power of the city of Bentre, "We had to destroy the town to save it."

Political liberty—indeed, politics itself—seems to be a luxury of the rich. *We* say that the quarrel is between Communism and capitalism. Whoever wants to meet the Communist argument has to argue not only political liberty, which most of us, and almost none of them, enjoy, but also capitalism, which, on the whole, in its socialistically modified form, operates successfully in a wealthy society like ours. If Communism is nothing but public ownership, or control, under government then we have a communist Post Office, a communist Social Security System, a communist school system, a communist military system, and a partially communist public utilities system. Nearly every other free country has, in addition, a communist transportation system, a communist communications system, and a largely communist banking system. The welfare state is a combination of private and public ownership, of capitalism and Communism, in accordance with Abraham Lincoln's dictum that the purpose of government is to do those things for the people which they cannot do as well for themselves.

Rather than confront the enemy at this level of hard argument, we find it less complicated to confine the quarrel to the issue of political democracy—which, say the Communists, is a fraud without economic democracy. The reason we prefer to avoid the hard economic argument is not simplification alone; in a deeper sense our avoidance stems from our inability to *believe in* capitalism. Capitalism, or *laissez faire,* is impossible to *believe in,* in a world where things are radically wrong. In a starving world it is impossible —for a people who spent for years more than a million dollars a day just to store their rotting agricultural surpluses—to defend the view that things should be left alone. Modified capitalism works sufficiently well under the peculiar American conditions (though thirty-five million Americans go to bed every night hungry, according to the late President Kennedy). But we do not and cannot believe in it as an article of moral faith.

The reason is that we ourselves are all communists—every one of us—in the most intimate and important of our associations. We are all members of families and every family is a truly communist organization, organized squarely on the communist doctrine of "from each according to his ability, to each according to his need." So, too, in our church and civic work, in our service clubs and our veterans' associations, and in our relationships as personal friends and good neighbors; in these activities there is no profit incentive compatible with sound capitalist doctrine, no self-interested motivation beyond the satisfaction of service.

The exalted commitment to communism (with a small "c") in the production and distribution of goods and services is binding no less upon every American than it is upon every Soviet citizen, and still more binding on the American who professes Christianity and regards his country as a Christian country. In the economic order, and without regard to evolution or the power state, there was in early Christianity a degree of communism: "Neither was there any among them that lacked; for as many as were possessors of lands or houses sold them, and brought the prices of the things that were sold, and laid them down at the Apostles' feet; and distribution was made unto every man according as he had need." (Acts 4:34–35) This was the economy of Christ's congregation in Jerusalem—a communism purer far than the Soviet Union's, where a man may own a private house and keep it.

"He who has a surplus has stolen it from his brother." Only compare these words of St. Francis with Proudhon, "Private property is theft," and say what the difference is between the saint and the atheist as regards economic justice. He who accepts Scripture is God's steward over property, and nothing more. He cannot be a Jew or a Christian and assert his *right* to the world's goods, or the supremacy of competition over co-operation, acquisition over sacrifice, or private property over public responsibility. "The atheists," says Dean Hromadka of Prague's Comenius Theological Seminary, "have had to descend upon us to remind us of the requirements of Christ and the prophets."

Of course the practice of Marxist Communism does not square with the theory. But what practice does? After almost two hundred years the theory of the Declaration of Independence has still to be practiced in many areas of our own national life. After fifty years Communism is yet to be practiced in the Soviet Union. We ask for time; so do they. We plead the progress we have made in two centuries; they plead the progress they have made in five decades.

The Russian under Communism has shoes and education. His grandfather had neither, and, if the present-day Russian does not have political liberty, neither did his barefoot, illiterate grandfather. When the Russian has had shoes and education as long as we have, he may, like us, demand and, like us, get political liberty. Meanwhile we Americans take comfort in the fact that even if Communism has provided the bare necessities of life, its application has been coercive and not free, and cannot, therefore, be compared with the family or the church. But the U.S.S.R. does not claim to be a family or a church. It claims to be a state, and all states use whatever degree of coercion they feel they need to maintain their security and—as have churches—penalize heresy. As the anti-Communist state coerces Communists, so the Communist state coerces anti-Communists, though admittedly to a greater degree.

Nor is the Soviet Union merely a state like ours, but one which is trying to carry forward a revolution. There is no blinking its periodic tyranny or the mass atrocities periodically committed in its name or its overt and secret encouragement of its own kind of revolution abroad. But these evils are not the invention or the peculiar pride of Communist revolutionaries. They are characteristic of social revolution at all times, everywhere. The fact that they occur under Communism—with its profound ideal of social justice—does not render them any less deplorable. But neither does it startle the student of human history.

We hear that there is the threat of Communist revolution all around us—and we see the example of it on our Caribbean doorstep. But we do not hear of such revolution in those few rich societies like our own, but rather in the abject poverty of countries in Latin America, Asia, and Africa. The number of right-wing dictatorships in Latin America, all of them single-mindedly dedicated to the prevention of Communism, increases. Why is there no threat of democracy in such countries? Why cannot the world's greatest salesman with the world's greatest product, and the balance of its power, sell democracy? The reason is that the poverty-stricken world's experience of democracy has been the experience of militarist tyranny and naked exploitation in the name of capitalist free enterprise.

What will save us, and our libertarian heritage, from the threat of Communist domination? What will save us—if we do not destroy ourselves in the name of anti-Communism—from the hungry Russians and the hungrier Chinese and the *still* hungrier "gooks" who surround us?

What may save us from the Communists—*though not from ourselves*—is human nature. In order to survive, without regard to external danger, the Communist society must produce the socialist new man whose appearance its propagandists herald. This new man will be socially and not individualistically dedicated, loving his neighbor as himself. Without him, Communism will never come to be, much less survive, but crumble from within and in its last agonies see capitalism re-emerge.

Capitalism makes do with the old man, sometimes known as the Old Adam, whose first interest is himself and whose last (as far as capitalism's requirements are concerned) is also himself. "Men are bad," says Machiavelli, and Adam Smith, in his *Wealth of Nations,* assures us that the baker and the butcher are motivated wholly by their own advantage and not in the least by the consumer's needs. "*Homo homini lupus,* Man is to man a wolf," says Sigmund Freud. By contrast with this pessimistic view of human nature, Communism has a utopian view of human nature. Marx saw man as by nature good, crippled by the bourgeois form of production and distribution. His emancipation—a favorite term with Marx—would follow inevitably from the overthrow of capitalism.

But there is no persuasive sign that it has or will. With the emergence of the new man, the state was to wither away; instead it flourishes with a bureaucracy unimaginable to the decadent capitalist societies. The new man has not yet made his appearance, in spite of some small and uncertain traces detected by observers in the degree of dignity represented by such phenomena as the rejection of tipping, the acceptance of the responsibility to labor, and the prevalence of community concern—phenomena explained in part by coercion of one kind or another.

If men are bad, the Communist jig is already up, its epitaph pronounced by the last of the Bonapartes when he heard of the Paris Commune: "So, they're turning over the dung-heap again." In replacing "mine" and "thine" with "ours," Communism presupposes the new man and is unthinkable without him. Without his materialization its cornerstone collapses and nothing but naked tyranny shores up the system in which, according to its great philosopher, "the free development of each is the condition of the free development of all." If man is not fit to be a Communist, he won't be. He will go through the motions as long as he has to, dragging his heels the while, and in the end come into the streets again, pick up the paving blocks, and put an end to the pretense and the pretenders.

But if men are good, or can by some means become good, then it would seem that Communism without coercion is inevitable, no matter where or how the line is held against it. But this is, so to say, where we came in two thousand years ago. Man outside the Garden was bad, having forfeited God's goodness. But he was still God's handiwork and still redeemable by God's grace. Through Christ he can be renewed: "If any man be in Christ, he is a new creature: old things are passed away, behold, all things are become new." (2 Cor. 5:17)

Without the hope of redemption and renewal man would try to live by bread alone, by the religion of economics, capitalist *or* Communist. And trying so to live, he would go on killing and dying in the struggle for bread—or for more bread. His good intentions would continue to pave and repave the road to hell. "They aim at justice," Dostoevsky's Father Zossima cries, "but, denying Christ, they will end by flooding the world with blood." "They"—and "we," including those who affirm Christ—have done just that since the first man (to use Marx's term) was "crippled"—not by this economic system or that, but by his own nature.

In the Christian view, the capitalist and the Communist are both right, and both wrong. The capitalist is right about man's being bad—and wrong in settling for badness and erecting a social system upon self-interest. For "in Christ" he can be good enough to be a communist; the old man, incorrigible through the First Adam, is corrigible through the second. And the Communists are right about his being corrigible—and mortally wrong in supposing that he can correct himself by his own unaided powers.

The challenge of Communism does not emanate from Marx, or from the Soviet Union, or from China, and it is not to be stopped by military means. The challenge of Communism is within us. And its failure, if it fails, is our own. Marx's error was the error of arrogance; his faith was in man. He, no less than we, marveled at the work of man's hands. If our faith in the perfectibility of man provides us with a power beyond our own—the power of God to lift us up individually and socially—we may have the hope of winning through. Without it, and with Marx's reliance on our own poor powers, "we" and "they" will continue to flood the world with blood.

5. WHAT CAN WE DO ABOUT IT?: Alternatives to Anti-Communism

THE POLICY OF A GREAT NATION must be based on certain positive criteria, both moral and strategic. What distinguishes the present era in world history from all others is that moral and strategic considerations now counsel the same choices. We live in a world where hundreds of millions of people seek social justice through revolutionary change, and in a nation where racial minorities and the poor are demanding what is rightfully theirs.

The aspirations of this great mass of humanity are the vital factor of the generation, and the nation that stands against those aspirations or tries to check or subvert them must lose ground until it is finally eclipsed as a great power. Even if we assume, for instance (as the authors of this study do not), that military power is necessary to contain Communism, it is quite obvious that our military power itself will be whittled away unless we take a moral stance toward the desire of people to better themselves in the developing nations as well as at home. It does the United States no good to form a military alliance with Iran and build bases there if the reactionary Shah who rules that nation is overthrown by a hostile populace. Nor can American policy, no matter what it is, succeed abroad if disaffected millions at home are burning down cities and conducting guerrilla warfare against a system that they feel has a false order of priorities. It will avail naught if the United States wins the arms race, subdues the National Liberation Front in Vietnam, and harnesses Latin America totally to its will, if the élan and the expenditures needed for such a policy convert the nation itself into a Bonapartist state.

Today, for the first time in history, the moral and strategical factors of policy coincide. In the nineteenth century when Britain held India or when it established a base in China by helping the Manchu dynasty suppress its people, its policy was immoral, but it paid off, it brought practical results for some in the form of great profits. Today such an approach is outmoded: No longer can a nation serve its own security interests by being exclusively self-interested and unprincipled in the means it employs. On the contrary, an immoral unwillingness to meet the rising expectations of the injured and oppressed will assure its decline as a great power.

It is from this perspective that we must judge the long term effectiveness of Communism and neutralism on the one hand, and America's anti-Communism on the other.

The Communist world has enormously expanded its influence since 1945, not by reason of the intrinsic soundness of such Marxist theories as surplus value or the law of immiserization, but because it has addressed itself to the real problems that lie underneath the swell of revolution—feudal and tribal social stagnation; colonialism; economic inequality; the need for land reform, education, and economic development; the demands of revolutionary nationalism. Communism may be the wrong answer, but it addresses itself to the right question—how to replace outmoded institutions that freeze the masses in poverty with dynamic ones that free them to ascend to a better life.

Anti-Communism, by contrast, has generally shied away from fundamental social change. We do not deny that the overwhelming majority of the economic and social projects financed by the United States through its various aid programs have been useful in themselves. When the American administration builds a university in Peru or sends midwives to India to teach modern obstetrical methods, it is performing a function that *by itself* is a good one. But if this aid buttresses a reactionary military clique and freezes atavistic institutions in Peru or India, its *effect* is not to solve but worsen the problems of the masses in those countries.

There have been exceptions to the rule, but by and large anti-Communism has not addressed itself to the real, insistent, and burning problems of the impoverished multitudes in Asia, Africa, Latin America, and at home. We have to choose between the alternatives of continuing our anti-Communist policies or adopting policies that are realistic and creative and that move in the direction of peace. To go on pursuing the mistaken policies of anti-Communism will only lead to disaster.

ARMAMENT FOR PEACE?

Inevitably and direfully the manufacture of arms provokes fear among other nations who seek, in turn, to lessen their fear by acquiring comparable weapons of their own. An armament race ensues. Since World War II we have witnessed the most expensive ballistic binge since the world began. Armaments have grown in cost, complexity, and destructive potential, spiralling through the stages of atom bombs, hydrogen bombs, rockets, and ballistic missiles. The latest advance is the antiballistic-missile system that is being actively promoted by the Chief of Staff in the Pentagon and the defense industries, who see a very good thing in a military gamble with stakes ranging from $5 to $40 billion. The decision of the government to build a "thin" ABM system at a cost of $5 billion is but a precursor of more to follow. The same military, industrial, political forces that pressured this minisystem into being will not rest content until the complete $40-billion system has been built. Yet other countries do not have the surplus to pay for this kind of security—and it would be criminal to try to force them to do so.

The mind is staggered by the enormity of military expenditures that are justified by a blind anti-Communism. These expenditures approached a trillion dollars for the United States alone over the last two decades. Economists have often pointed out that armaments are nonproductive as well as counterproductive. Once built, armaments add nothing to the economy. They plow no fields, they harvest no crops, they construct no machinery and no buildings. They create no income once they have been made, unless they can be peddled abroad to countries without the technology to make their own weapons.

Once the weapon rolls off the end of the assembly line, it becomes a nonproducer. The magnitude of military spending measures the extent to which defense has become a growth industry. Hence in the United States a loose alliance has arisen between the makers of arms and the user of arms that has been called "the military-industrial complex." This complex invades every area of American life; it is a built-in feature of our economy which embraces all of us, whether we work on an assembly line, behind a delicatessen counter, or as a bond salesman. We are all merchants of death.

It is unconscionable in face of the world's needs that enormous funds should be poured into creating, supplying, and maintaining the military build-up of poor nations in exchange for their promise of assistance to keep Communism in its place. World needs continue to multiply, and the increase of arms does nothing to alleviate these needs. Altogether too much foreign aid has been military aid.

It has been estimated that national defense outlays now use up $150 to $200 billion in world resources annually. Of this, $120 billion or more annually is spent by the U.S.S.R. and the United States, largely in mutually offsetting deterrence. Shocking sums are devoted to holding back the efforts of the poor to break out of their oppression. And yet the prospects of these people appear so hopeless that a Congressman, George E. Brown, said "I believe that most Americans would resort to the same revolutionary violence if confronted by the same problems." [1]

Arms Sales and Arms Aid Abroad

Armaments aggravate world tensions, and yet the United States has become the world's leading anti-Communist arms merchant. In addition to what we sell are vast quantities that we give away. Formerly this was not the case. In the fiscal years 1952 to 1961 the United States military grant aid program amounted to $17 billion, and $5 billion in sales were chalked up. According to Defense Department estimates for the 1962–72 period, only $7 billion will be grant aid, and sales will total $15 billion. [2]

The economic horror of these armament sales to underdeveloped countries becomes clear when we think of the tremendous social needs in those regions. The whole gamut of national development is embraced by the needs of societies striving to enter the twentieth century. That money which could otherwise raise a people's standard of living should be put into guns indicates a false order of priorities. The United States should play no part in such a gross misappropriation of funds.

Among the developed nations our best cash customer has been West Germany, which in the last four years has bought $3 billion worth of military equipment. The sale of these arms has aggravated East-West tensions. For the Soviet Union has been very sensitive to a rearmed Germany, remembering her past invasions by German armies. The transactions were demanded by American policy makers because the dollars earned helped offset the cost of our troops there. In view of the fact that there are one-half million West German troops, it is at least arguable that American troops are not needed, and the sale of arms should cease.

Bad though it is to sell weapons that perpetuate the Cold War, and reprehensible though it be that arms sold in the name of anti-Communism to underdeveloped countries divert cash sorely needed for schools, health, and development, even worse is the fact that often the weapons are given to military cliques who use them to maintain their power. It is imperative that underdeveloped countries move ahead quickly and bring about urgent reforms and de-

[1] *The Nation*, "I'm Tired of Your Gimmicks," December 11, 1967, p. 616.
[2] From a staff study of the Senate Foreign Relations Committee published in *Current*, August 1967, pp. 33–41.

velopment. If radical social change threatens their position of power, the oligarchies brand all its advocates as Communist subversives and use these arms to quash civilian unrest.

Far more aid has been given to dictatorial regimes that would grant military bases to the United States (Franco, the Latin-American dictatorships, Chiang Kai-shek, Thai leaders, Ky and Thieu in Vietnam, the Shah of Iran, and many others) than to regimes that would not. Even in granting help to a neutral nation like India, the overriding concern has been: Will this aid keep the nation out of an alliance with the Soviet or Chinese bloc? The basic interest of the Indian people has been a secondary consideration.

In 1954 the most egregious example of American interference took place in Guatemala. Here a Communist-supported regime headed by Jacobo Arbenz came to power. Among the inexcusable acts of Arbenz had been to expropriate holdings of the United Fruit Company. The Central Intelligence Agency set about to overthrow it—and gave arms and planes to a reactionary local group to do so. This is a flagrant but by no means isolated instance of the use of American arms to intervene in the internal affairs of Latin America.

Military dictatorships are the rule in Latin America; not infrequently their officers have been trained in the United States and their weapons are marked "Made in U.S.A." It is not the avowed intention of the United States to thwart social progress; indeed, we have publicly affirmed an Alliance for Progress in South American countries. However, where progress has involved tampering with American investments in those lands, then social betterment has been vetoed, and United States arms have been used to buttress dictatorship.

The day is past when we can be guided merely by such narrow concepts of national self-interest. In an interrelated world, progress will have to be conceived in world terms rather than parochial terms. The world cannot forever be divided between the rich nations and the poor. The poor will not tolerate it; *world* development is imperative.

Sabre-rattling is not the way to save American investments. When Mexico nationalized its oil industries, it was able to negotiate agreements with United States concerns that reimbursed those concerns over a period of years for their loss. Other Latin-American countries could do the same and their social development could proceed. It is chastening to recall that Castro wanted to work out some financial agreement to reimburse American concerns for properties

108 ANATOMY OF ANTI-COMMUNISM

he planned to nationalize, but the United States turned a deaf ear to his request.

We must realize that the underdeveloped countries need to undergo radical social change and they must not be stymied by an American phobia that brands all efforts to change the status quo as "Communism." We must stop foisting military aid on poor nations struggling to improve the life of their people, and we must bring a halt to our military and moral support of military dictatorships that stand between the people and a restructured society that will begin to meet people's needs.

Thus anti-Communism not only fails to respond to the true problems of the present world, but regrettably it has strengthened the very elements—the dictators and conservatives—who cannot and will not deal with those problems. Moreover, the dynamic of relying on dictators and conservatives, for the purpose of military containment, leads to a situation where world nuclear war becomes well-nigh inescapable. The dictator relies on our military aid to retain his power; he uses it to suppress his people and when his people rebel, we intervene with more military aid and military training, the internal war escalates, and we finally intervene with our own Green Berets and eventually our own forces as in Vietnam. As we write these words there is only one Vietnam on the horizon, but there are incipient Vietnams in Bolivia, Nicaragua, Venezuela, Aden, Saudi Arabia, Brazil, the Dominican Republic, Guatemala, Peru, Colombia, and other places.

This is not merely our private opinion but a conviction increasingly voiced by others knowledgeable about world affairs. So Dr. Richard Shaull, who served as a missionary in Brazil, writes after a recent extensive trip throughout Latin America in which he met with a wide variety of people who represent the potential leadership of that part of the world: "We are headed directly for a number of new Vietnams in Latin America, in which U.S. military power will be used against these young people who are willing to sacrifice their lives to build a new social order, many of them being outstanding representatives of a new generation of Christians." [3] Nowhere have events gone as far as in Vietnam, but they veer in the same direction.

There, concomitant with our military aid and military intervention, the "other side" sends aid to the nationalist forces fighting

[3] *The War of National Liberation: Next Stage in Latin America*, Dr. Richard Shaull, Latin American Department, Division of Overseas Ministries, National Council of Churches, September 1967.

against the American ally. Each step leads to a counterstep, each escalation to counter-escalation, each lapse of morality to further lapses of morality, until the great powers confront each other at the brink.

THE ARMS RACE

Risking World War III

Policies of anti-Communism risk World War III. Back when the atomic age was only five years old, on March 1, 1950, Brian McMahon, Senator from Connecticut, spoke on the Senate floor to urge his colleagues to promote peace. His words are still relevant and come to us with even greater urgency now, nineteen years after they were first spoken.

With each swing of the pendulum the time to save civilization grows shorter. When shall we get about this business? Destiny will not grant us the gift of indifference. If we do not act, the atom will. If we do not act, we may be profaned forever by the inheritors of a ravished planet. We will be reviled as cowards—and rightly—for only a coward can flee from the awesome facts that command us to act with fortitude. This time of supreme crisis is a time of supreme opportunity. The prize of atomic peace lies waiting to be won—and with it a wondrous new world.[4]

There is nothing new that can be said about the nuclear jeopardy in which we live out our days. We live in what has been termed "the age of overkill" where the United States and the Soviet Union have amassed sufficient atomic weapons to kill every living inhabitant of the earth several times over. The number of stockpiled nuclear weapons represents a lethal potential that staggers the imagination. The mind cannot cope with the casualties implied by such a storehouse of death. And, for his own psychic health perhaps, modern man has blocked out of his consciousness the horrendous holocaust that would be entailed in World War III.

At this moment there are only two nations that have the power to bring the world down in nuclear ruin, the Soviet Union and the United States. Both countries demonstrated a recognition of this power in their handling of the Middle East crisis of 1967. There seemed to be a studied attempt, arising from mutual fear, to avoid a military confrontation. But in their relationship there must be

[4] Quoted in Richard J. Barnet, *Who Wants Disarmament?*, p. xvii.

more than the respect of each for the power of the other. It is vain to think that this alone will preserve the peace. If beneath the "balance of terror" there is a profound contempt, then there will be schemes to outwit the other and to bring about his destruction. Thus, early in the atomic age there were those in Washington arguing for preventative war against the U.S.S.R., just as there are those urging the same against China today.

Since war, especially in the nuclear age, is the epitome of irrationality, it is foolish to imagine that if war breaks out between the United States and the Soviet Union, reason will prevail. It will not. But the successful avoidance of war in the long run will depend upon a reduction of the hostilities that exist between the two giants. Their mutual responsibility for sparing the world a nuclear hell had already begun to result in a new détente, which has been seriously strained by the Vietnam War. In the face of the world situation, anti-Communism is an irresponsibility that cannot be allowed to fan the flames of suspicion in a world that is a tinderbox.

Years ago Albert Einstein observed: "The unleashed power of the atom has changed everything except our way of thinking. Thus we are drifting toward a catastrophe beyond conception. We shall require a substantially new manner of thinking if mankind is to survive." We can no longer think in terms of a military victory that is no longer possible. We must abandon the idea of defense; there is none against nuclear bombs. *We must choose.*

A generation ago, two generations ago, what upset the balance of world power was usually the rival economic interests of the great powers themselves. What upsets the world balance of power today is national revolution that has economic consequences. The Communists and a host of nationalists and other types of radicals have attached themselves to this national revolution; anti-Communism, by its military emphasis and its dynamic of self-interest, has detached itself. The result has been that the United States, never more strong economically and militarily, faces one crisis after another that it is unable to resolve. Never in its history has its security been so threatened as it is today; the very expenditure of $900 billion on the arms race has made it not more secure but less so, for in relying on the many dictators who have incorporated as part of the free world alliance, we are undermining the basis of our security and its moral rationale. Anti-Communism is its own worst enemy, for it will not assure American victory or stability.

but will surely lead to American decline, despite the combined, fearsome power of its airplanes and nuclear weapons.

With this understanding, it seems to us that American security depends on joining with, rather than standing against, the revolution of rising expectations. British historian Arnold J. Toynbee speaks for many thoughtful non-American observers of the world scene when he writes: "America is today the leader of the worldwide anti-revolutionary movement in defense of vested interests." [5] The choice that determines our future he sees clearly: "Is she for social justice, or is she against it? I believe it would be no exaggeration to say that the United States' answer to this question, whatever the answer may be, is going to be decisive for her fate." [6]

The anti-Communist policy must be jettisoned and a new democratic-revolutionary policy formulated. Whether we like it or not, the world of tomorrow will be far different from today's. It does not lie within the American province to decide whether it will be Communist or anti-Communist (reactionary), but only whether it will be revolutionary and democratic or revolutionary and totalitarian. The wisest defense of America's security, therefore, demands a thoroughly moral concern for the long-term interests of the poverty-stricken world community as well as the downtrodden here at home. It is not only in the religious sense that we have an obligation to the poor, but in the strategic one that if we do not help others to help themselves there is no hope for our own survival. Starvation and political oppression create revolutionaries around the world; those revolutionaries fight for national liberation and, in the process, upset the world balance of power leading inevitably to war. Anti-Communism, by failing to apply the preventative medicines that these revolutionaries need, by failing to change oppressive institutions, exacerbates international tensions and takes us inevitably toward the mushroom cloud of holocaust. The foundation of strategy for the United States must lie in the substitution of a democratic revolutionary alternative for the antirevolutionary alternative of anti-Communism.

Anti-Communism obscures basic issues; it misleads us into a false understanding of what the major world problems are. It persuades us that a vicious ideology is all that stands between us and entrance into paradise: Just let the minions of this political, eco-

[5] Arnold J. Toynbee, *America and the World Revolution,* New York, Oxford University Press, p. 92.
[6] *Ibid.,* p. 209.

nomic, and religious heresy be struck down, and all will be well. We need to replace the fallacies of anti-Communism with attitudes and policies that are designed to advance humanitarian ideals.

De-escalation of Military Expenditures

It is imperative that military outlays be de-escalated. An arms race cannot be carried on indefinitely. The highly sophisticated armaments that have now been amassed are in continual danger of bringing about a war by accident. No official assurances that such a thing could never happen can be fully persuasive. One recalls the electric failure that plunged the northeastern portion of the United States into total darkness in 1965, or two navy planes that on August 21, 1967, were shot down over China. The planes possessed highly advanced navigational equipment and yet strayed seventy-five miles off target, due apparently to the failure of electronic components.

The reduction of armaments on the way to total disarmament would reduce tension between the United States and the Communist world. Although every nation protests that its weapons are merely defensive in intent, other nations are not inclined to believe them. The experiences of the United States ill prepare it to appreciate the anxiety of Russia and China over its own military stance. The United States has not been invaded for 150 years. Yet both China and the U.S.S.R. have been invaded repeatedly, and they regard the armaments that ring their borders with a skepticism born of bitter experience.

One can seriously question whether attempts made at disarmament heretofore have been sincere. Each side has been willing to surrender something it considers nonessential to its own defense while demanding a sacrifice that its rival considers essential to security. The ideal of a general disarmament remains a utopian and visionary dream while the arms race proceeds apace. A mutual distrust frustrates the dismantling of military hardware. How does one create trust where none exists?

Only an act of trust can create trust, only a decisive and imaginative venture in statesmanship can end the vicious circle of armament and rearmament, of threat and counterthreat. With its massive aggressive and retaliatory power, the greatest in the world, the United States is obviously in a position to initiate the reduction of terror. There is no guarantee that such an act would evoke a pacific response from the Soviets. We do know though what the alternative entails, for we have seen its consequences over the last twenty years in the power struggle between the United States and the Soviet Union. The creation of military power by one has been matched by the other. That road leads but one place: ruin.

There is good reason to believe that the Soviet government might welcome a scaling down of the armaments race. There are vast consumer needs in Russia that are still unmet, and there is an increasing internal pressure to see that these be met. If the resources now going into weapons were reallocated to meet these needs, the change would be received enthusiastically by Soviet citizens. Soviet-produced weapons are as sterile economically as American-made bombs, and probably housing needs alone would absorb the billions of rubles now spent for military might. So long as the arms race continues, these construction projects remain thwarted.

It may be that domestic needs of the United States are less than those in the Soviet Union, but this is debatable. Although our technological development has taken place over a longer period, we have also created more problems for ourselves thereby. For example, there is the grim joke about the man who fell into New York City's East River; he didn't drown, he was polluted to death. The pollution of our rivers and streams and lakes and air is a problem of such immensity that there are not even knowledgeable estimates as to what their purification would cost. It has been said that it would take hundreds of billions of dollars to refurbish our major cities. We need 700,000 classrooms, hospitals with a million beds, eight million housing units, new mental institutions, and other social facilities.

These are only suggestions of the problems that face America in area after area, and it is not possible to postpone grappling with them into the indefinite future. They will worsen with neglect. America must resolve these problems while they are still of manageable proportions, but this will never be done so long as our preoccupation with Communism syphons off, for military purposes, funds that are desperately needed in more constructive projects.

And what is true for the United States and the Soviet Union is overwhelmingly true for the underdeveloped countries of the world. They cannot afford our wars, or even our preparation for war.

ALTERNATIVE ATTITUDES

Communism Will Not Disappear

The change of attitude that the times require of us is perhaps best illustrated by the case of China. It is now obvious, twenty years after the Chinese Communists gained control of China, that Chinese Communism is not going to disappear. No matter how the "great cultural revolution" is concluded, the political and social institutions of almost a quarter of the human race will not revert to their pre-Communist form. As Ronald Steel observed about China: "She will be a great power even if Mao Tse-tung and his comrades should turn in their party cards and sing hymns to Adam Smith." [7] And there is no more chance of that than of the Pentagon becoming a peace society, so we need to recognize the permanent necessity of adjusting to a decisive change in this huge, awakening society.

Communism is firmly rooted in other lands too. For many years after the Russian Revolution, many outside that country greeted every indication of unrest within it as a harbinger of the day when the Russian people would rise and throw off the Communist rule. It was an idle hope. Communism in the lands where it is now established will change; but it is highly improbable that Communism will vanish.

We must accept the fact that Communism is here to stay. Relations between Communist and non-Communist societies will have to evolve during a long period of adjustment and accommodation. There are sharp differences of understanding between us that make dealings difficult. It is a foolish fantasy, however, to imagine that some fine spring morning we will awaken to discover that Communism went away with the snow. It will not, nor should we feel so confident or arrogant that our opposition will contain, reverse, or overthrow Communism. There are limits to American power and influence.

Emphasis on People

The foreign policy of the United States should be directed toward the welfare of people, whoever they are, wherever they are. In 1963 President Kennedy appointed a committee to review foreign aid. This committee found that after the Marshall Plan, out of $50 billion of foreign aid expenditures, $30 billion were spent directly on military equipment. "Of the remaining $20 billion, about 85 per cent was also military in that these funds were made available to support the budget of nations mainly on the periphery of the 'Iron Curtain' that have undertaken a scale of military effort far greater than they can afford." [8] Economic aid was a small

---

[7] Ronald Steel, "The 'Yellow Peril' Revisited," *Commentary*, July 1967.
[8] *The New York Times*, international edition, April 5, 1963, quoted in David Horowitz (ed.), *The Free World Colossus*, p. 215.

portion of the total amount. The emphasis upon military alliances and the fashioning of bulwarks to contain Communism is often at the expense of social progress.

The same problem of priorities that the United States faces in the allocation of its funds is intensified in the developing lands. There the social deficits are much greater; many of these societies are only beginning the long climb into modernization. They need industry, they need schools, they need roads, they need dams, they need hospitals, and much more. The funds that go into armaments are snatched away from desperately needed measures toward human progress. Even worse, it aggravates problems that are not static but grow as population increases widen the disparity between developing and highly industrialized states.

We need a foreign policy that will set its criteria by how well the people fare in land after land, a foreign policy that has humanitarian aims. The removal of poverty on the world level is even more urgent and imperative than the end of poverty in the United States. The hopeless of every land will look to a violent answer to their problems where none other is forthcoming.

It is impossible for the average American, surrounded by affluence, to understand the needs and aspirations of the multitudes of the poor. We live in a world apart. Our abundance and their deprivation never touch. Our superfluity of things insulates and isolates us from their need. But we must try to appreciate what underdevelopment means for the two billion human beings who suffer under it, for only an awareness of their condition will make us realize that radical, revolutionary social change alone will better those conditions.

Robert Heilbroner, in a vivid illustration, has helped us do this. He imagines how a typical American family, living in a small suburban house on an annual income of six or seven thousand dollars, could be transformed into an equally typical family of the underdeveloped world.

He begins by stripping their house of its furniture. Everything goes except a few old blankets, a kitchen table, a wooden chair. Each member of the family may keep in his "wardrobe" his oldest suit or dress, a shirt or blouse. Only the head of the family may keep a pair of shoes, but not his wife or children.

The appliances have already been taken from the kitchen. Of foodstuffs and supplies, everything goes but a box of matches, a small bag of flour, some sugar and salt, a handful of onions, and a dish of dried beans. A few moldy potatoes, already in the garbage

can, must be rescued and will provide much of tonight's meal. All
the rest of the food is removed; the meat, the fresh vegetables, the
canned and frozen goods, the crackers, the candy.

The house has been stripped, the bathroom has been dismantled,
the running water shut off, the electric wires taken out. Next take
away the house. The family can move to the toolshed, where it is
crowded, but much better than the situation in Hong Kong, where
(a United Nations report tells us) "it is not uncommon for a family
of four or more to live in a bedspace, that is on a bunk bed and
the space it occupies—sometimes in two or three tiers—their only
privacy provided by curtains." [9]

This is only the beginning. All the other houses in the neighborhood have also been removed; our suburb has become a shantytown. Still, our family is fortunate to have any shelter at all; 250,-
000 people in Calcutta simply live in the streets.

Our family is now about on a par with the city of Cali in Colombia, where, an official of the World Bank writes, "on the one
hillside alone, the slum population is estimated at 40,000—without
water, sanitation, or electric light. And not all the poor of Cali are
as fortunate as that. Others have built their shacks near the city,
on land which lies beneath the flood mark. To those people the
immediate environment is the open sewer of the city, a sewer which
flows through their huts when the river rises." [10]

Still, to reduce our American family to the level at which life is
lived in the greatest part of the globe, all communication must go
next. No more newspapers, magazines, books—not that they are
missed; our family would be illiterate. In our shantytown we will
allow one radio, which is generous since the national average of
radio ownership in India is one per 250 people, the majority of
them owned by city dwellers.

Now government services must go. No more postman, no more
fireman. There is a school, three miles away and consisting of two
classrooms. But the classes are not overcrowded; only half of the
children in the neighborhood go to school. The community has no
hospitals or doctors. The nearest clinic is ten miles away, tended

[9] "Social Aspects of Urban Development," Committee on Information from
Non-Self-Governing Territories, March 10, 1961, quoted in Robert L. Heilbroner, *The Great Ascent: The Struggle for Economic Development in Our
Time*, p. 34.
[10] "The Cauca Valley," unpublished World Bank memo by George Young,
quoted in Heilbroner, *op. cit.*, p. 35.

by a midwife. Unless the family has a bicycle, which is unlikely, the hospital can be reached by bus—not always inside, but there is usually room on top.

Finally, money. We will allow our family a cash hoard of five dollars. This will prevent our breadwinner from experiencing the tragedy of an Iranian peasant who went blind because he could not raise the $3.94 that he mistakenly thought he needed to secure admission to a hospital where he could have been cured.[11]

The head of our family, as a peasant cultivator with three acres of land to tend, may raise the equivalent of $100 to $300 worth of crops a year. If he is a tenant farmer, which is more than likely, a third or so of his crop will go to his landlord and probably another 10 per cent to the local moneylender. But there will be enough to eat. Or almost enough. The human body requires an input of at least 2,000 calories to replenish the energy consumed by its living cells. If our displaced American fares no better than an Indian peasant, he will average a replenishment of no more than 1,700 to 1,900 calories. His body, like any insufficiently fueled machine, will run down, one reason why life expectancy at birth in India today averages less than forty years.

The children may help, if, fortunately, they find work and thus earn some cash to supplement the family's income. And if not? Well, they can scavenge as do children in Iran who in time of hunger search for undigested oats in the droppings of horses.

So we have brought our typical American family down to the very bottom of the human scale. It is, however, a bottom in which we can find, give or take a hundred million souls, a billion of the world's people. Of the remaining people in the backward areas, most are slightly better off, but not much so; a few are comfortable; a handful rich.

Of course, this is only an impression of life in the underdeveloped lands. It is not life itself. There is still lacking the things that under-development gives as well as those it takes away: the urinous smell of poverty, the display of disease, the flies, the open sewers. And there is lacking, too, a softening sense of familiarity. Even in a charnel house, life has its passions and pleasures. A tableau, shocking to American eyes, is less shocking to eyes that have never known any other. But it gives one a general idea. It begins to add pictures of reality to the

[11] *The New York Times Magazine*, April 30, 1961, quoted in Heilbroner, *op. cit.*, p. 36.

statistics by which underdevelopment is ordinarily measured. When we are told that half the world's population enjoy a standard of living "less than $100 a year" this is what the figures mean.[12]

This is the world with desperate, revolutionary needs—the world in which Americans find revolution so distasteful, so subversive, so "Communistic."

Meeting Domestic Needs

One of the tragic consequences of our militaristic anti-Communist crusade is the diversion of money from desperate areas of need in America. Despite its enormous wealth, the United States does not have unlimited resources. We have to acknowledge as a nation that if we choose to do this with our money, it means we cannot do that. The billions of dollars now spent on so-called national security are diverted from more fruitful programs. According to Senator Fulbright, since 1946 we have allocated more than $1,578 billion through the regular federal budget. Of this amount, some $964 billion or 61.09 per cent has gone for military purposes, less than $96 billion or 6.08 per cent has gone for social purposes. The American people need to establish a more rational and healthy sense of priorities for our national goals.

The scale of the opportunities before us is enormous. It has been estimated, for example, that American national security outlays in 1964 were deflecting some $46 billion worth of resources from other uses, and that even if $6 billion were contributed to an international security organization and $9 billion retained for possible minimum defense programs for internal security, roughly $31 billion would be available for redirection.[13] At the present price levels, and with escalated Vietnam outlays, the figure would be more like $50 billion.

Numerous careful studies in recent years have shown conclusively that the resources freed by reduced arms spending need not stand idle—that with sensible and feasible arrangements during a transition period, they could be shifted to a variety of other uses.[14] In a similar vein, other recent studies have spelled out in detail the great opportunities for meeting pressing needs that will be avail-

[12] Heilbroner, op. cit., pp. 23–27.

[13] See Emile Benoit and Harold Lubell, "The World Burden of National Defense," in Emile Benoit (ed.), Disarmament and World Economic Interdependence, p. 54.

[14] See, for example, Wassily Leontief, "The Economic Impact—Industrial and Regional—of an Arms Cut," Chap. 10 in his Input-Output Economics, pp. 184–222.

able from the steadily growing output potential of our economy. Wise and prudent economic policies will permit us to use massive resource increments in pursuit of the ends we consider vital.

High priority should clearly be given to the festering sores of our society. There is a tremendous need to provide jobs. The Report of the National Advisory Commission on Civil Disorders pointed out there are 2 million unemployed with about 10 million underemployed and 6.5 million who work full time and earn less than the annual poverty wage. It is imperative that we upgrade our inner-city schools, where Negro students fall farther behind whites with each year of school completed, and where, despite the overwhelming need, less money is spent educating ghetto children than the children of suburban families. It is urgent that we improve our welfare system by raising the level of assistance on the one hand and eliminating demeaning restrictions on the other. The condition of our cities is a national scandal, for in them lives 56 per cent of the country's nonwhite families, nearly two thirds of them in substandard housing. Adequate housing must be built.

Add to these needs the need to conserve and replenish our natural resources, including the purification of water and air, and the regional development of distressed areas. They add up to important and valuable goals making an enormous demand upon our national budget. And we must get our priorities right.[15]

It is not possible to have guns and butter, despite administrative assurance to the contrary. President Johnson's 1968 budget message gave dramatic witness that the financial requirements of war demand the curtailment of social legislation. The tremendous claims on America's resources will not be met so long as we are preoccupied with building military walls of containment against Communism's influence. The $70 billion that in 1967 went into our defense budget are dollars that cannot be used for new schools, new housing, expanded medical care for the poor, or a dozen other urgent national needs. The diversion of money into arms makes our problems worse, by postponing their solution.

Relations with China

One rallying cry of anti-Communism is to regard any Communist regime as an implacable enemy, a social pariah, a moral leper with whom contact should be avoided, whose existence must be officially

[15] The nation's needs and opportunities are regularly discussed in the *Annual Economic Report of the President,* together with the *Annual Report of the Council of Economic Advisers,* transmitted each January to Congress.

ignored. So it was sixteen years after the Russian Revolution, on November 16, 1933, that the United States finally recognized the government of the Soviet Union. It has now been nineteen years since the Chinese People's Republic was founded, but the United States still refuses to face the fact of China's existence. There is no profit in pretending that what exists does not. The solid truth is that mainland China is under the effective control of a Communist government. How much longer can the United States engage in the game of make-believe? Nearly fifty members of the United Nations have diplomatic relations with Communist China, and there is no diplomatic reason why the United States should not be among them. Without such diplomatic conversations our relationship cannot improve. Serious students of the Far East have warned that if the United States and China continue to pursue their present policies, they are on a collision course. With China pressing forward to develop its nuclear capacity, such a consequence could be a global disaster. It is of the utmost urgency that we reverse our policy of implacable hostility toward China.

Perhaps diplomatic relations would have to await the growth of other relations such as trade. Again, other nations have not been prevented by an anti-Communist bias from doing so. Trade of non-Communist countries with mainland China in 1964 exceeded 2 billion dollars worth of goods. Today Japan is one of China's leading suppliers. Neither former hostilities nor ideological differences are allowed to stand in the way of their commercial transactions. Canada has sold large quantities of wheat to China. The San Francisco Chamber of Commerce has called for opening the doors to trade with China. It is obviously in a good position to gain much if this were done, yet the whole country has much to gain, not merely from an economic standpoint but in a diplomatic sense as well.

Trade is not simply the exchange of goods and cash. It is correspondence, telephone conversations, business trips. It is the intermingling of men with one another. There is an urgent need for Chinese and Americans to come to know one another as human beings with similar emotions, aspirations, and needs. During the last generation, years of stress, each has come to regard the other through the lens of Capitalism or Communism and what each perceives is an ideological caricature of a genuine homo sapiens. These distortions exist in the absence of countervailing and corrective personal encounters.

It is highly unfortunate that at a time early in the history of relationships between the Chinese Communist government and the United States when China would have admitted American newsmen, the U.S. State Department refused its permission. Now the situation is reversed: The United States is willing to allow visits to China by certain selected personnel such as journalists and medical specialists, but there has been no indication of their welcome on the part of China. Still the difficulties in initiating these visits does not detract from their value. Every diplomatic channel should be employed to see whether a way can be opened for the beginning of personnel interchange between citizens of the most populous nation of the West and the giant of the East.

We live in a world that is a militarized camp. Both Russia and China have complained that their borders are ringed with American armaments. One need only look closely at a world map to see that the charge is substantially true. American missile sites, troop deployment, airfields, and naval installations are indeed to be found on the peripheries of China and the Soviet Union. The converse is not true, although Russian submarines equipped with missiles hover around our coasts even as ours remain within target distance of theirs.

It is amazing how insensitive Americans are to the reaction of the Communist countries to their encirclement. One need only think back to the time of the Cuban missile crisis and remember what anxiety went through the United States. How can we account for American blindness that fails to see a similar reaction among Russians and Chinese to the presence of American military might on their borders? How would we feel if Chinese troops were in Canada or in Mexico, as near our borders as we are to theirs? How would we react to a Chinese fleet off the shores of California or patrolling the approaches to Staten Island? Are we so convinced that we are moved only by the noblest of motives, that we cannot conceive that our actions are open to less benevolent interpretations?

What would American response be if Soviet missiles sat poised in Canada; if Chinese troops, airfields, and naval bases were located in Mexico? It is questionable whether American hysteria could be controlled short of embarking into World War III. Yet, as Senator J. W. Fulbright observed once, "We have treated the constant Soviet preoccupation with our overseas bases as sort of an unreasonable Soviet obsession." [16] It is not an obsession at all. It

[16] Quoted in D. F. Fleming, *The Cold War and Its Origins, 1917–1960*, Vol. II, p. 1076n.

is a very understandable human reaction to a threat, a reaction we in the United States would make if the situation were reversed. In fact, this was our reaction at the time of the Cuban missile incident.

The de-escalation of the Cold War against the Soviet Union and China could begin with a dismantling of the armed rings around them. Even from the point of view of military strategy they no longer serve the purpose they were intended to serve.

Western Europe has become strong, both economically and politically. She no longer needs an American military shield twenty years after World War II. The vigor and diversity of political trends in Eastern Europe no less than in Western Europe makes the old fears of a disciplined, obedient, centrally organized Communist machine, capable of seizing continental power, a figment of obsolete imagination. Most Europeans have been far swifter in recognizing this new situation than have Americans.

We have become accustomed to overlook its absurdity, but if we could achieve a degree of objectivity, if we could look afresh as though for the first time, as a visitor from another planet, we would be struck by the tragic absurdity of the present state of non-relationship between China and the United States. Here is nearly one quarter of the human race that we have chosen to ignore because we dislike their form of government. Despite our phenomenal news gathering equipment, our TV cameras, tape recorders, short-wave radios and all the rest, our information about China is limited to what a few China-watchers sitting in Hong Kong are able to piece together from monitored newscasts out of China, interviews with travelers from China, and perusal of Chinese publications. The sooner normal relations are established between China and the United States, the better will be the future for the world. Chiang Kai-shek is not going to reconquer China; the present Communist leadership of China, despite internal struggles, is not going to be soon deposed by pro-Western leaders; the revolution will continue, and the United States may as well become reconciled to the way things are in China and see whether communication can be restored between East and West. The world we save may be our own.

Full diplomatic relationship may be resumed only after the United States has granted China full diplomatic recognition. To suggest, as opponents of such a move have, that recognition somehow inevitably carries with it moral approval is mistaken. The United States recognizes many governments which it does not morally approve of: South Africa, Portugal, Spain, the Soviet Union, and Yugoslavia, for example. The attempt to withhold recognition from China as an instrument of political pressure has to be judged a failure, and a more fruitful and realistic policy must take its place.

Serious questions have rightly been raised about the United States stand of opposition to the seating of Communist China in the United Nations. Some of our staunchest allies have disagreed with this stand. One of the most important of these is India, China's neighbor, who would have much to lose if China should prove to be the fire-eating dragon the United States has often pictured her to be. In June 1957 Secretary of State Dulles, in justifying the United States campaign to exclude mainland China from membership, said "the United Nations is not a reformatory for bad governments," and contended that the seating of Peking would "implant in the United Nations the seeds of its own destruction." [17]

The problem of Nationalist China's seat will have to be resolved; it will not be easy, but it is not insurmountable. What is lacking at this point is the American will to see mainland China take its rightful place within the United Nations. Whether a "two China" policy could be worked out that would satisfy all parties has not been sufficiently explored.

China's entry into the United Nations, might, in fact, be disruptive. One hopes that the United Nations could remain intact while trying to contain radically opposed members. This, however, is not the real issue. Nor is the issue whether China would refuse to accept membership. The issue is whether China is entitled to membership, and whether she could be invited to join. To this we offer an unequivocal "Yes." Yes, even though the Chinese Communists might conduct themselves with more vigor than finesse.

The fires of revolution tend to cool over a period of time as fervent enthusiasm declines from fever pitch. This is so not only because some limited objectives of the revolution are realized but also because there emerges a generation that knows nothing of the conditions that provoked the impulse to revolt. The sweep of history engenders confidence that time will exercise the same restraint in the case of China as it has with Russia.

It is not just a matter of arteriosclerosis of conviction. As living conditions are improved, a growing number of people have a stake in the status quo that they wish to preserve. Hence they are loath to embark on rash actions that might place in jeopardy the values that have been gained. We have seen this happen in the case of the

[17] Quoted in A. Doak Barnett, *Communist China and Asia*, p. 447.

Soviet Union with the resulting cleavage between that country and China. We have every reason to believe that, if she prospers, China will walk down the same road the Soviet Union has walked into the temperate zone of international relations. It is our task to help make that transition as swift and free of explosive potential as possible.

Our problem with China is not her revolution but her hostility toward foreigners, exacerbated by American hostility to the point of xenophobia.

We make a mistake, however, if we think that by military means we can effectively limit China's influence on Southeast Asia. By its sheer bulk, it will be a predominant factor in directing what takes place in that part of the globe. Bombs and military might can in no way prevent the knowledge of China's daring social experiment from affecting the attitudes of the underdeveloped peoples seeking to bring themselves into the twentieth century. The contention that China's major attempt to influence its neighbors will be by military aggression has little evidence to support it.

China has had border disputes with India, Pakistan, and the Soviet Union. The ground for these disputes was in part laid by British colonialism—and even Chiang Kai-shek agrees with mainland China on these issues. By negotiation or force China took back what had been nominally hers for centuries. Having done so, she sought no further gains. True, China speaks in harsh and warlike terms at times. Lacking another kind of deterrent force, she employs what has been called "verbal deterrence."

When it comes to Russia, it must be conceded that every direct, human contact that we have been able to have with her has been beneficial, allowing the warmth of human relationship to thaw the Cold War a little. Those devotees of anti-Communism who have opposed cultural exchanges with the Soviets are blind to the human dimensions of peace. Study conferences, scientific meetings, professional exchanges, visits of churchmen, all have values in revealing to the participants a humanity deeper than the ideological differences. Political enmity may be just a trifle more difficult to maintain once the "enemy" becomes a personal friend.

The current effort to expand trade relations between the United States and the Eastern Communist bloc must be applauded. Trade contributes to a nation's self-esteem and well-being. As its trade is enlarged, so is its interest in maintaining that trade. National hostilities disrupt trade, and nations are prone to pacify differences in order that trade can be resumed.

Righting Racial Wrongs

There is a certain irony in that, while we fight for freedom abroad, we deny it systematically to a neglected portion of our citizens at home; that while we profess to be striving to reconstruct societies abroad, we trifle with the reconstruction of our own deteriorating cities. Part of the problem is economic. Money that buys bombs for Vietnam cannot be used to buy bricks for urban schools. As Martin Luther King, Jr., put it: "The bombs in Vietnam explode at home: they destroy the hopes and possibilities for a decent America." [18]

It is estimated that we spend about $322,000 for each "Communist" we kill in Vietnam (three out of four of whom are civilians), whereas in the so-called war on poverty, we spend approximately $53 for each person classified as poor. Our obsession with "Communism" has led us away from the urgent needs at home. We must reverse the process.

It has been estimated that to remove the substandard housing from our cities and to replace it with adequate housing represents a capital expenditure of trillions of dollars. It is in the face of such overwhelming need of our own people that the gross immorality of our expenditures in Vietnam to defeat Communism becomes apparent. The housing deficit is bad enough in itself, but it is also a symbol of neglect that carries over into other areas including education, vocational training, recreation. As long as these pressing needs go unmet we can expect the riots that have erupted in our cities to increase in frequency and furor.

Those who clamor for more police protection and a multiplication of the means of controlling unruly crowds largely miss the point. They are proposing to deal with the consequences of a problem and overlooking the source of that problem. In scores of our large cities, for example, there are hundreds of thousands of high school dropouts, and high school graduates, who have never had a job. They are jobless, for one thing, because the jobs they might have had in other years, unskilled jobs, are rapidly disappearing. For another thing, many of these youths have a high school diploma, but they have been cheated. The diploma does not really represent a high school education. They grow up in ghettos, disadvantaged before they began school, and still disadvantaged when they finished, several grades behind in actual achievement. They

[18] Martin Luther King, Jr., *Where Do We Go From Here: Chaos or Community?*, p. 86.

represent, in James B. Conant's phrase, "social dynamite." We are accumulating a social debt that will someday have to be paid.

Fear and hatred understandably lead to attempted repression of mobs through strong police action, sealing off and beating down the unruly minorities and their protests. Law and order in urban ghettos are sought through riot control methods, using fire hoses, tear gas, night sticks, and guns in crowded residential communities. The response has come increasingly in the form of rocks, Molotov cocktails, and sniper's bullets—a tragic and profoundly irrational detour from the right road. The unemployed need jobs. The unskilled need training opportunities. Parents want education for their children. Decent families want decent housing. The lawless and disorderly are precisely the jobless, unskilled, overcrowded people whose legitimate claims appear to be falling on deaf ears. If the demands for justice of our minorities are not met, they will increasingly turn toward violence.

The Support of Freedom

Our leadership of the free world would gain more in credibility if we evidenced more ardor in doing something about the repressive regimes of Spain, Portugal, Rhodesia, and South Africa. If the denial of individual liberty, which we profess so disturbs us about Communist government, is really a concern of ours, then we should show a similar concern when non-Communist governments reveal a lack of sensitivity toward those who differ politically or racially from those in power. Economic pressures could be exerted against these repressive nations to move them toward greater freedom.

A group of experts appointed by the Security Council of the United Nations reported to the Council that economic sanctions against South Africa could be effective if universally applied. This confirmed the conclusions of the International Conference on Economic Sanctions against South Africa held in London in April 1964, "that total economic sanctions were politically timely, economically feasible and legally appropriate." [19]

In the Security Council debate on economic sanctions, the argument was made that such sanctions would bear most heavily on the nonwhites. In response, the delegates from Morocco read a statement of 11 June, 1964, by Chief Albert Luthuli appealing to all governments throughout the world, to people everywhere, to

[19] *United Nations Doc. s/P.U.1129,* June 10, 1964, pp. 8–10, quoted in *International Conciliation,* November 1964, p. 110.

organizations and institutions in every land and at every level, to act now to impose such sanctions on South Africa that will bring about the vital necessary change and avert what can become the greatest African tragedy of our time.[20]

Neither the United States nor the United Kingdom showed much enthusiasm for the idea, inasmuch as both have sizable investments in South Africa. As of the end of 1961 the United Kingdom had about $2.256 billion and the United States over half a billion, which has since increased considerably. The UN is still studying the question. If the United States wants to do something for the cause of human freedom in the world, it might reconsider its policy relative to South Africa.

Yet another place in Africa where freedom is hard pressed is in the Portuguese-held territories of Angola, Mozambique, and Portuguese Guinea. In order to resolve the problems in those areas peacefully, the United Nations Security Council in July 1963 outlined a policy reaffirmed by the General Assembly. The Council urgently called upon Portugal (1) to recognize immediately the right of the inhabitants of all the territories to self-determination and independence; (2) to stop repressive measures and withdraw all military forces; (3) unconditionally to grant political amnesty; and (4) to negotiate with nationalist groups "with a view to the transfer of power" leading to immediate independence. Other nations were requested to refrain from offering Portugal any assistance, including arms and military equipment, that would enable it to continue its repressive policies.[21]

Very little has been done in carrying out these recommendations. The offending nation maintains an army of fifty thousand Portuguese troops in Angola, twenty-seven thousand in Portuguese Guinea, and an estimated forty thousand in Mozambique in order to keep the nationalist elements in each colony under subjection and keep the drive for independence from spreading to uncontrollable limits. In 1967 Portugal had a defense budget of $188 million, reflecting a 33 per cent increase over 1966, an indication that it intends to continue the suppression of the nationalist forces in its colonies.

Here then is a situation in which the United States could exercise some moral leadership—it could show to the world that it does indeed stand for the right of a people to determine its own destiny.

[20] *Ibid.*
[21] *United Nations Doc. S/5380,* July 31, 1963.

This would seem to provide an area where the United States, instead of being pitted against the Communist bloc of nations, could co-operate with them in bringing about the end of antiquated colonial domination. There is no valid reason why the United States should find itself in opposition to the Communist world where the protection of subjugated peoples is the point at issue.

National Aid on a Basis of National Reform

To facilitate this, aid should be given to a nation on the basis of its willingness to proceed with rapid nonviolent social change aimed at raising the living standards of its masses and enlarging the freedom of its citizens. The upgrading of national life should include such projects as: (1) land reform; (2) the organization of co-operatives; (3) the initiation of programs to lift the levels of education, medical care, and housing; (4) the extension of civil liberties; (5) the involvement of the people in the decisions of the political process; and (6) the reduction of the gap between the rich and poor segments of society.

A basic problem in all the underdeveloped lands is that most of the land is owned by a few of the people. The landless peasants make up the bulk of the population. They till their plots by the sufferance of the landlords, who exact high rent in the form of a percentage of the crop and charge high interest on money borrowed between harvests. Social change must begin by correcting this ancient injustice, by seeing that the worker of the soil has a vested right to the land he farms.

The underdeveloped countries are essentially rural and unorganized as far as the commercial interest of the peasant is concerned. By teaching them the rudiments of marketing and distribution, we could help them to form co-operatives. They would be enabled to make more economical purchases of their seed and agricultural supplies; they would expand their cash crops and begin the long climb out of destitution.

The social deficiencies in the underdeveloped countries are staggering. Educational facilities are minimal, illiteracy prevalent. Some idea of the medical needs can be gained from statistics for life expectancy in emerging nations. Most of the inhabitants of these nations are born, live, and die without ever being seen by a physician. The housing needs are incredible. The migration into cities has been a world-wide phenomenon, and the resulting slums and congestion pass belief.

The granting of civil liberties has been a rather tardy entrant into the movement to humanize the relationship between government and people. The Bill of Rights is amendments to the U.S. Constitution, not part of the original, and the struggle for civil rights still goes on in this country. In many underdeveloped nations civil liberties exist in embryo. The ruling classes often rule with a heavy hand. Dissent is discouraged, and not infrequently it is brutally suppressed.

The worst features of life in emerging nations will move toward solution as the people are drawn into the governmental process. The base of decision-making might be broadened to include eventually the entire citizenry. This cannot take place at once. An elite must rule perhaps until the majority can be educated to take their place. Yet the concentration of power into the hands of an elite minority can be disastrous to the public welfare. The minority may exercise its power for its own benefit, not that of the nation, and social betterment becomes possible when the influence of the majority becomes dominant in political affairs. It is at this point that aid from outside can be helpful by insisting that financial grants are conditional on social change calculated to better the life of the masses, and insisting on the masses' gradual participation in political and economic decision-making.

The tremendous injustice in land ownership in most underdeveloped lands reflects the profound gap between the rich and the poor. The great body of wealth is owned by a comparative handful of people. They control the government and they are deaf to the needs of the people. The masses of the people are penniless. Their aspirations and hopes will remain illusory until they are given more financial stake in their society. Government projects and industrialization can provide employment and money.

The meanings of terms like "democratic" are not absolute. The legislative and executive structures can vary widely from one society to another depending on each people's heritage. For our purposes here, a democratic regime will be considered one that does not need to apply force against its people, beyond the local police role of maintaining the rule of law; that does not enforce an environment which seriously smothers the creativity of individual citizens; and that constantly seeks to increase the widest political participation of the people. Democracy is both social (for example, schools and clinics) and economic (for example, increased earnings), and progress in undeveloped nations must be judged primarily by these criteria of democracy. In a democratic society, the majority does not carry its policies to a point where a dissenting minority must be brutally suppressed. By the same token, contending forces in the society feel a sufficient sense of common interest so that they cease using guns against their opponents. We observe that democratic societies, defined this way, are not feasible today in some parts of the world. Where they are feasible, the labels of "socialist" or "capitalist" that may apply to their institutions seem to us less crucial than the characteristics of their performance outlined above.

How can nations be encouraged to take their primary steps to social progress? It is proposed that aid to these nations be contingent upon their adoption of those projects calculated to raise them out of their economic and political doldrums. It could be argued that the ruling parties in such countries would never consent to the voluntary liquidation of their personal kingdoms. They could see the handwriting on the wall and know their days were numbered if these projects were carried out. On the other hand they might become persuaded that it was impossible to sweep back the rising tide of expectation and, if they knew no military aid would be forthcoming to help maintain them in their positions of privilege, they might see that in their case too the strategic and the moral course coincide. Anyway, the ruling elite, without our military aid, would, above all, be vulnerable to removal by its own people.

The social change envisioned is not mere tinkering with the machinery of state but thoroughgoing, radical, nonviolent change. Nothing less should be acceptable; nothing less will be tolerated by the world's masses. They have starved long enough; they have been deprived of necessities that others have in abundance. They know now this does not have to be. There are going to be radical social changes in our world. The only question is whether they will be in some degree orderly and according to some schedule or whether they will be violent, convulsive, and painful. The question, we repeat, is not whether there is to be change or no change. There will be radical change, the status quo is doomed. The world moves toward greater justice. The question is, How will it be achieved? Who will provide the economic wherewithal to induce these revolutionary changes in the underdeveloped countries?

Even if the United States had limitless resources, which it does not, it would be inadvisable for us to extend the needed aid unilaterally. Such aid would be and has been used to buy friends. The main motive for the aid then becomes, not the welfare of the country helped, but America's narrow self-interest. Underdeveloped countries are quick to sense, and resent, being used in this way.

Aid to nations in need should be multilaterally given. The United Nations is the obvious agency through which these funds should be channeled. This removes the suspicion that support is being sought for one nation's policies. It also helps create what is so critically needed, cooperation among diverse nations. National competition and conflict must give way eventually to international cooperation. The beginning has been made in the UN, but only the merest start as yet. World anarchy must be replaced by world law, and again the United Nations is a faint flicker of light.

Multilateral Aid

We should rapidly move away from bilateral aid arrangements toward multilateral groupings both on the giving side and on the receiving side. If rich countries join together in providing economic assistance, their ideological motives can be muted, and it will be far easier for sensitive nationalist governments to accept the aid. Without predicting overnight success, we would suggest that it will be far easier for Eastern European countries and the U.S.S.R. to join such an international effort, perhaps through United Nations channels, than to make joint efforts with the United States alone. If we think of the world as increasingly the basic community for all men—as the authors of this paper think we must—and if we follow the analogy of the present national states, then it is not too far-fetched to propose that contributions to an international aid fund be assessed, for example, in proportion to the gross national product of each nation.

If bilateral arrangements were replaced by grouping of aid-receiving countries, following the Western European precedent of Marshall Plan days, there would be many healthy consequences. Where now a sensitive new government in a traditional society is highly resentful of the advice and performance standards imposed along with United States economic aid, it could far more readily accept equivalent discipline imposed mutually within a group of receiving states. Pressures for necessary institutional changes would be far more acceptable coming from fellow-reformers working at similar problems than from the rich uncle with a very different heritage.

The emphasis on aid focuses attention on the real problem, human need, rather than the imagined one, Communism. If it is true, as the authors of this paper contend, that the real threat to humanity's future is ignorance, disease, hunger, human exploitation, and exploding populations, then the favored nations must address themselves to these problems, and warfare against these *conditions* is the only kind of warfare that promises a future for mankind.

If American economic assistance, pooled with that from other developed countries, were passed to a group of recipient nations for division among themselves, one could even visualize competition in discipline as a consequence. A recipient member of the group whose political turbulence and administrative malperformance eroded its claim to a share of the available assistance would be under strong pressure to discipline itself. Fellow recipients capable of using assistance effectively could claim their shares on logically and morally defensible grounds. The climate for healthy and effective development, free of lurid ideological Communist and anti-Communist claims, would be far more propitious. It is now generally recognized that many very poor economies face extremely difficult problems, that rapid success is impossible, and that frustrations will be painful. We propose no panacea. We do suggest, however, that an anti-Communist outlook which uses unilateral economic assistance as an instrument for fighting international Communism should be abandoned for a more effective approach.

In conclusion, the anti-Communist mentality exacerbates an already tense relationship with the Communist world. It denies the humanity of Communists, and it feeds the emotions that spiral the arms race. Being irrational, it renders a rational judgment on Communism impossible. It is a phobia that cannot countenance the development of cordial relations with the Communist or neutralist world. And so it must be replaced with saner attitudes that make possible more creative, peaceful approaches to build bridges across the ideological chasm that separates the United States from the Communist-neutralist portion of the globe.

Once we recognize that revolution is not imposed by outside agitators, that it is an honest response to the needs of an undeveloped society and indeed may be a necessary precondition to modernization, we may see our way to dealing with it in a way that is consonant with our own long-term interests. What is needed is not counterinsurgency but *competition* with the Communist world. If we could shift our overriding concern from anti-Communism to pronationalism, we would enter into competition with China and the Soviet Union for leadership of the forces of modernization. In the short run those who stand to gain from such a policy are the peasants and the nation-builders of the Third World. In the long run the United States would win the fruits of leadership of the peoples of the world in seeking mutual solutions to the problems that increasingly bind us together in one common human destiny.

SELECTED BIBLIOGRAPHY

ALPEROVITZ, Gar, *Atomic Diplomacy: Hiroshima and Potsdam.* New York, Simon and Schuster, 1965. The use of the atomic bomb and the American confrontation with Soviet power.

BARNET, Richard J., *Who Wants Disarmament?* Boston, Beacon Press, 1960.

BARNETT, A. Doak, *Communist China and Asia.* New York, Vintage Books, 1961.

BELL, Daniel (ed.), *The Radical Right.* New York, Doubleday, 1963.

BENOIT, Emile (ed.), *Disarmament and World Economic Interdependence.* New York, Columbia University Press, 1967.

BROAD, Lewis, *Winston Churchill, A Biography.* New York, Hawthorn Books, 1958.

EBENSTEIN, William, *Today's Isms: Communism, Fascism, Capitalism.* Englewood Cliffs, N.J., Prentice-Hall, 5th Edition, 1967.

EISENHOWER, Dwight D., *Mandate for Change, 1953–1956: The White House Years.* Garden City, N.Y., Doubleday, 1963.

FLEMING, D. F., *The Cold War and Its Origins, 1917–1960,* 2 vols. Garden City, N.Y., Doubleday, 1961.

FULBRIGHT, J. William, *The Arrogance of Power.* New York, Vintage Books, 1966.

HEILBRONER, Robert L., *The Great Ascent: The Struggle for Economic Development in Our Time.* New York, Harper & Row, 1963.

HOFSTADTER, Richard, *The Paranoid Style in American Politics.* New York, Knopf, 1965.

HOROWITZ, David, *The Free World Colossus.* New York, Hill and Wang, 1965.

HOROWITZ, David (ed.), *Containment and Revolution.* Boston, Beacon Press, 1968.

KENNAN, George F., *Russia and the West.* Boston, Atlantic-Little, Brown, 1961.

KING, Martin Luther, Jr., *Where Do We Go From Here: Chaos or Community?* New York, Harper & Row, 1967.

LAFEBER, W., *America, Russia and the Cold War.* New York, John Wiley, 1968. Contains excellent bibliography.

LENS, Sidney, *The Futile Crusade: Anti-Communism as American Credo*. Chicago, Quadrangle Books, 1964.

LEONTIEF, Wassily, *Input-Output Economics*. New York, Oxford University Press, 1966.

PECK, Graham, *Two Kinds of Time*. Boston, Houghton Mifflin Co., 1950.

RIEBER, Alfred J., *Stalin and the French Communist Party, 1941–1947*. New York, Columbia University Press, 1952.

SNOW, Edgar, *The Other Side of the River: Red China Today*. New York, Random House, 1962.

STEEL, Ronald, *Pax Americana*. New York, Viking Press, 1967.

The War in Vietnam, prepared by the Staff of Senate Republican Policy Committee. Washington, D.C., Public Affairs Press, 1967.

WILLIAMS, William Appleman, *The Tragedy of American Diplomacy*. Cleveland, World Publishing, 1959.

MEMBERS OF THE WORKING PARTY ON
Anatomy of Anti-Communism, AFSC

James E. Bristol has been on the staff of the American Friends Service Committee since 1947 and an AFSC representative in Zambia in 1965–66. Former Director of the AFSC Program on Nonviolence and pastor of Grace Lutheran Church in Camden, New Jersey, he was imprisoned from 1941 to 1943 as a conscientious objector to World War II. He is co-author of *Speak Truth to Power* and *In Place of War* as well as the author of pamphlets and magazine articles.

Holland Hunter has taught at Haverford College since 1948. The author of *Soviet Transport Experiences,* he visited Russia in 1957, 1959, and 1966. He is also the co-author of *Economies of the World Today.*

James H. Laird served as pastor of Central Methodist Church in Detroit from 1958 to 1966. Since 1962 he has written a column on religion and current events in the *Detroit Free Press*. He is a co-author of *The Draft?*, the former Director of Working Party Studies for the American Friends Service Committee, and currently Executive Secretary, the Social Concerns Committee, the Philadelphia Yearly Meeting, the Society of Friends.

Sidney Lens lecturer, world traveler, trade union leader, is the author of *Left, Right and Center; The Counterfeit Revolution; A World in Revolution; The Crisis of American Labor; Working Men; Africa— Awakening Giant; The Futile Crusade: Anti-Communism as American Credo;* and co-author of *In Place of War.* He has contributed articles to numerous journals in the United States and abroad and traveled in eighty-one countries, lecturing at many universities and from many public platforms.

Milton Mayer calls himself an unemployed newspaperman. A prize-winning journalist, holder of the George Polk Memorial Award and the Benjamin Franklin Citation, he has long written for leading periodicals in America and abroad. Mr. Mayer has also served on the faculties

138 MEMBERS OF THE WORKING PARTY

of the University of Chicago, William Penn College, Frankfurt University in Germany, and the Comenius Theological Faculty of Prague and is currently teaching at the University of Massachusetts. His study of Nazism, *They Thought They Were Free: The Germans 1933-45*, has been republished as a paperback. His most recent book is *What Can a Man Do?*

Robert E. Reuman has taught at the University of Pennsylvania and Temple University. He has traveled widely, doing relief work for the American Friends Service Committee in China from 1949 to 1951 and acting as Director of the Quaker Student House in Freiburg, Germany, from 1951 to 1953. Currently he is associate professor of philosophy at Colby College.

Athan Theoharis taught at Texas A & M from 1962 to 1964. From 1964 to 1968, he taught American history at Wayne State University. Currently he teaches at Staten Island Community College in New York. His specialization is twentieth-century American history. Author of *The Yalta Myths: An Issue in American Politics, 1945-55*, he is at present completing a book on the political origins of McCarthyism.

Bryant Wedge Director of the Institute for Study of National Behavior at Westminster, Massachusetts, was formerly Psychiatrist in Chief of the Department of University Health at the University of Chicago, later holding the same position at Yale. He was U.S. Eisenhower Exchange Fellow in 1958-59 and is the author of *Visitors to the U.S. and How They See Us* as well as numerous articles and pamphlets.